Flying Scared

Flying Scared

Why We Are Being Skyjacked and How to Put a Stop to It

ELIZABETH RICH

STEIN AND DAY/*Publishers*/New York

For Ross and Ginny

First published in 1972

Library of Congress Catalog Card No. 70-127227

Published simultaneously in Canada by Saunders of Toronto, Ltd.
Designed by Bernard Schleifer
Manufactured in the United States of America
Stein and Day/*Publishers*/7 East 48 Street, New York, N.Y. 10017
ISBN 0-8128-1356-1

Preface

FIRST OF ALL, let me say that I have never been skyjacked. Nor do I want to be skyjacked. I do admit to a preoccupation with the subject, since I am an airline hostess as well as an author. When I first started flying in 1963, skyjackings were infrequent occurrences which flight crews considered more puzzling than threatening—a freak crime soon forgotten once the small flare of publicity had died down. It wasn't until 1968, which yielded an alarming crop of twenty-one skyjackings, that any of us seriously considered Havana as a possible destination when we went out on a flight.

Even then, the crime seemed bizarre and titillating. Sensational press coverage—planeloads of passengers being whisked off on an unexpected side trip to Cuba—provided the armchair traveler with vicarious thrills. There was an absurd air of festivity surrounding the crime as each incident terminated safely in Havana. The key word here is "safely"; anyone seriously considering the potential for tragedy inherent in skyjacking could only regard the prospect of a skyjacking epidemic as alarming.

The year 1969 holds the unenviable record for skyjacking: 92 worldwide, 42 of them involving United States planes. But by the end of 1971 there had been over 335 skyjackings, some 130 of them involving United States planes. And of these 130 incidents 75 percent took place between 1969 and 1971.

These figures are roughly accurate, give or take ten or so skyjackings; reports from various official agencies contradict each other as to just how many there have been. Skyjacking being such a public and spectacular crime, it doesn't seem unreasonable to assume that it would be a simple matter to agree on an accurate count. But in fact, this is just a minor example of how people and governments differ among themselves on just about every aspect of skyjacking.

In any case, numbers don't really tell us much more than that skyjacking has reached near-epidemic proportions, despite the efforts of airlines and law-enforcement agencies to control it. And it is the threat of a potential skyjacking disaster *that hasn't yet happened* that makes some of us hold our breath. Hopefully, governments can come to some rational agreement to stop skyjacking before the numbers become irrelevant compared to one major tragedy.

Taking the larger view, as they say in officialdom, the number of skyjackings is fairly insignificant in proportion to the thousands of flights scheduled each day. Statistically speaking bad weather and mechanical problems constitute a far greater hardship to the airline industry than does skyjacking. From a purely economic view skyjacking is a big nuisance—if you want to look at it that way, as one high official of the International Air Transport Association apparently does. "Oh, I don't think skyjacking is a serious problem, is it?" he said to me. "It seems to be going away." He didn't even add, "I hope."

In the five weeks following that conversation there were six skyjackings. A convicted murderer was talked out of skyjacking to Cuba by a hostess on her first flight. An Ecuadorian airliner was skyjacked, details unknown. The second 747 and the first United States plane carrying sky marshals was skyjacked to Cuba—by a man using a ball-point pen and a comb wrapped in a sweater—and held for three days in Havana with passengers and crew. A Canadian skyjacking was thwarted in midair when a crew member bashed the offender with a fire ax. After being given $200,000 and four parachutes, a skyjacker forced a plane to take off with its tail door open, out of which he disappeared somewhere between Seattle and Reno. And three men charged with murdering a policeman diverted a plane to Cuba.

Not only was the crime not "going away," more twists were being added. I can only hope that the IATA official was taking notes.

In the past two years skyjackers appear to have declared open season on airplanes and passengers, escalating an already tense situation by committing other crimes such as political blackmail, extortion, sabotage, kidnapping, and murder along with the crime of skyjacking. As this trend becomes more and more evident, somehow the news stories aren't so entertaining anymore.

I first became interested in the subject of skyjacking back in the days (by comparison, the good old days) when skyjackings from the United States were seemingly routine diversions to Cuba. My curiosity focused on what sort of person would commit the crime. Digging through the meager and often contradictory information available didn't bring much enlightenment in that respect. Interviews with government officials revealed an interesting and unexpected chronological history of skyjacking, but only the most superficial knowledge about the offenders. United States skyjackings continued in the same old pattern, and I began to suspect that the only way I was ever going to find out about what made a skyjacker tick was to be involved in a skyjacking. Hardly a desirable mode of research.

On September 6, 1970, I was on a layover in Chicago. The phone rang while I was putting on my uniform for a flight to Paris: "Miss Rich, this is your crew call for Flight 881. Do you have any warm-weather clothes with you?" I said No and waited for the news that we were being sent to Athens instead of Paris.

"Four planes have just been skyjacked to the Middle East. You never can tell where you're going to end up these days."

Unsettling, to say the least. Then, at our briefing that evening the captain offered this unexpected bit of information: "If anyone throws a grenade at you, pick it up and drop it in the lavatory—you have approximately seven seconds. There would at least be a chance of survival."

While one hostess was making a nervous joke—"The front lav or the back lav, sir?"—I was considering the nightmarish possibilities: rushing from one occupied lav to another, carrying a hot pineapple as the precious seven seconds ticked away. Lavs are always occupied when you need one the most.

In the anxious weeks that followed the Palestinian skyjackings I began spending more and more of my time trying to find answers to the new questions they raised. I interviewed people, sifted through files and books and documents, and at last was able to interview some skyjackers. In short, I became a skyjacking freak.

This book is the record of my journey around and through skyjacking territory—a shadowy land inhabited by people who are fully as bizarre as their behavior. I reluctantly add that the airline and government officials closing in on that territory don't always have the most rational reactions either. In fact, skyjacking seems to be a subject that unravels that lunatic fringe decorating some part of all our psyches. Nietzsche wrote a warning a long time ago which should have been posted before this all began: "He who fights monsters should beware that in the process he does not himself become a monster. For, if you look long into the abyss, the abyss looks also into you."

1

A PROSPEROUS-LOOKING southerner stepped up to a stewardess during a flight, stuck a gun in her ribs, and demanded to see the captain. Upon being ushered into the cockpit he made an announcement: "Ah'm hah-jacking this plane to Miami."

The captain looked around in amazement and said, "But this plane *is* going to Miami."

"Don't kid me, mistah," said the Texan. "Ah've taken this flight twice this month, and both times we ended up in Cuba. *This* time we're going to Miami!"

That is about the best skyjacking joke I have heard, and it isn't exactly a thigh-slapper.

Skyjacking [1] is not a subject that people joke about very well, and those who joke about it around airports are likely to find themselves apologizing to those notoriously humorless fellows, the FBI and other arms of the law. Very often I find that a mention of my own interest in skyjacking can produce near rabid reactions on the part of some passengers and harassed airline personnel.

Skyjacking is, of course, a subject clouded by hysteria and fear. Since the majority of United States flag carriers have been skyjacked to Cuba, the existing political tensions between the two countries led much of the public to stereotype the skyjacker as a wild revolutionary or a desperate criminal with pinko tendencies. The opinion I hear most often today is, "Just let us catch a few and send them to the electric chair, then this nonsense will stop." Commies and criminals being synonymous terms in many minds, the finer points of any argument get lost in the hue and cry of "Kill them."

Contrary to popular belief, skyjacking did not begin with political cranks forcing United States planes to Cuba, nor did the Cuban government establish the principle of "political asylum" for skyjackers—that diplomatic sacred cow which has stood in the way of any international agreements providing for the return and legal disposition of skyjackers.

A close look at the history of skyjacking reveals that the possibility has been with us, at least in theory, practically since the beginning of commercial aviation. A Ronald Colman movie called *Lost Horizon*, made in the 1930's, told the story of a planeload of passengers hijacked by its pilot to a paradise far removed from the insanity of World War II. And the first recorded incident of air piracy took place in Peru in 1930: a group of rebels commandeered a Pan American Ford trimotor and forced the pilot to land at Arequipa, where a revolution was in progress. The rebels intended to use the plane to distribute propaganda leaflets over the territory, but the British government was able to intervene and secured the release of the plane and crew after several days. The incident was forgotten until the pilot of the flight, Captain B. D. Rickards, was involved in another unsuccessful skyjacking attempt in July, 1961.

The first *successful* skyjackers took off from Romania in August, 1947, and landed in Turkey. This skyjacking was also the first to involve violence; one of the crew members was killed when he tried to disobey the skyjackers' commands. Next, in April, 1948, the United States was involved politically in a skyjacking when a Czechoslovakian airliner was forced to land in the United States zone of West Germany by thirty Czechs, three of whom were crew members.

There were nineteen recorded skyjacking incidents, successful and unsuccessful, from 1948 to 1958, the majority of them coming from Communist to non-Communist countries (only four of the nineteen were in the reverse direction). Although three of these skyjackings from East to West involved the murder of crew members and security guards, there is no record of any skyjacker's having been prosecuted in the West.

In view of recent events it seems surprising that the Cubans were bitten by the skyjacking bug first. Within Cuba Castroite guerrillas succeeded in two out of three skyjacking attempts on Fulgencio Batista's Cubana Airlines during 1958. On January 11, 1959, Fidel Castro seized political control of Cuba, and the United States granted political asylum to the first Cuban skyjacker on April 16, 1959. This "welcome" became standard procedure in the next few years: the precedent of political asylum for skyjackers had already been established by Turkey, by the United States Command in Germany, by Austria, Italy, Yugoslavia, Greece, Denmark, West Germany, and North Korea—a mixed political bag to be sure. Apparently not one of these countries doubted that skyjacking was a politically motivated act and, therefore, a justifiable one.

The United States had quickly become disenchanted with Castro's political tactics and socialist economic measures which wiped out, without a by your leave, sizable American business investments. Thousands of Cubans, equally disenchanted, were pouring into the United States, mostly from boats but occasionally from airplanes.

By the end of 1961 eight incidents of Cuban aircraft diverted to the United States had been reported in the press. (Some seventeen must have slipped in unnoticed; according to a statement by President John Kennedy in August of that year, the total was twenty-five.) The United States proceeded to complicate the skyjacking problem by seizing at least nine of the Cubana Airlines planes and selling them to satisfy American business claims against property nationalized by the Castro government.

So long as the United States remained on the receiving end of the skyjacking maneuvers, the issue seemed pretty clear-cut. America was opening her arms and embracing political refugees, if not huddled masses, from oppressive totalitarian regimes. True, she was satisfying a few Cuban debts in the process, but how could she be anything but pleased to help out these courageous people who would risk their lives (to say nothing of the other passengers' and crews') for political liberty?

Castro, following the example of the Eastern European countries in his response to skyjacking, added security guards to all commercial flights. They dealt viciously with all skyjackers. There are a few reports of unsuccessful Cuban skyjackings—inevitably violent—and probably more that went unreported in the press. Skyjacking was as politically embarrassing to Castro then as it is now to the United States, which at that time was complacently enjoying Castro's discomfort and costly measures to prevent the loss of his airplanes.

Up to 1961 there had been thirty-four successful and unsuccessful skyjackings worldwide. Fifteen of them had involved violence and fatalities; two of the fifteen planes had crashed. But since the blood shed was usually Communist blood, the Western powers did not pause to consider that they might be condoning and even encouraging a particularly unhealthy expression of political dissent. Certainly no one bothered to investigate the possibility that some of these skyjackers' motives might be more pathological than political.

No speculation on that front occurred until the United States was faced with *Americans*—political dissidents, it was assumed—forcing aircraft to Cuba. On May 1, 1961, the country was stunned by the news of the first skyjacking to Havana. The immediate public reaction was, "Crazy, why would anyone want to do a thing like that?" Anyone who wanted to was free to leave the United States at will, and there were legal ways for people to reach Cuba through other countries.

A Puerto Rican Castro sympathizer armed with a knife and gun had entered the cockpit of a National Airlines plane flying from Marathon, Florida, to Key West and ordered the pilot to fly to Cuba. When the plane landed in Havana, he told the Cubans that he wanted to warn Castro of an assassination plot and that he had brought the plane along to compensate for the Cuban planes kept by the United States. News stories added an imaginative touch discovered after the skyjacking—the name written on the man's ticket was Elpirata Confrisi, a famous eighteenth-century Caribbean pirate.

Castro seemed as perplexed by the incident as was the United States, and under the circumstances he acted more diplomatically than the United States had over Cuban skyjackings. Although "Confrisi" was granted political asylum, the plane, crew, and passengers were released the same day.

The second skyjacking to Cuba, on July 24, 1961—considered another freak incident at the time—was remarkable only for the fact that Castro caught on to the game and kept the airplane. Congress was in an uproar over Castro's "seizure of our plane," an Eastern Airlines Electra, conveniently forgetting that the United States had established the rules of the game. Castro eventually made his point, however; some months later the United States gave up the practice of selling Cuban aircraft and politely returned all aircraft subsequently skyjacked.

At the same time, the United States government committed what can only be considered (with the benefit of hindsight) a major diplomatic blunder: an offer from Castro to enter into a bilateral agreement for the return of both aircraft and skyjacker was ignored. (It is of historical interest that this proposal was also advanced by Ché Guevara at the Inter-American Economic Conference at Punta del Este, Uruguay, in August, 1961.)

Although the United States finally reached an agreement with Castro for the return of the Electra in exchange for one of his hijacked patrol boats, the situation obviously wasn't considered serious enough to warrant negotiating with Castro on an equal basis. Thus passed a chance to discourage skyjacking from the United States to Cuba and, perhaps, demonstrate the only truly effective means of dealing with the problem.

Cuba was left no choice but to follow the established precedent of political asylum for skyjackers. In the early sixties when no one—least of all Castro—foresaw that skyjacking could become an epidemic in the United States, each case seemed to be treated individually by the Cubans. When a Pan American flight was forced to Havana on August 9, 1961, by a French citizen of Algerian birth who had been living in the United States, the situation was hopelessly confused. To make it more embarrassing, the Colombian Foreign Minister to the United States was a passenger. Castro hurried to the airport to confer with the diplomat—a rare opportunity, since Cuba and Colombia had severed diplomatic relations some months earlier. Castro, quoted as saying, "This should not happen again," allowed the aircraft, crew, and passengers to return to the United States. The skyjacker was found to have had a history of mental illness, and Castro deported him to Mexico.

During the same period another skyjacking had been thwarted when the tires of an airplane were shot out by the FBI at El Paso, Texas, where it had landed to refuel. This skyjacker also had a history of mental illness, and his story contained an even more puzzling detail. On a trip to Mexico the week before, he had been granted permission by the Cuban Embassy there to emigrate to Cuba legally. He also had enough money to buy passage to Cuba from Mexico. Why on earth had he traveled back to the United States and then attempted to skyjack? The unanswered question caused a great deal of official anxiety.[2]

This unexplained link between the skyjacker and Cuba previous to the skyjacking attempt led the public and a number of congressmen to conclude that all skyjackings were part of a Cuban conspiracy. Congress answered this threat by promptly passing a law making air piracy a crime punishable by death or life imprisonment. Since no *commercial* United States aircraft were skyjacked in the next four years, it was assumed that the threat of the death penalty had taken care of those Commies, criminals, or crazies—whatever they were; so long as they stayed off airplanes, nobody much cared.

Nobody, that is, except Castro, who had his own conspiracy paranoia to contend with. Two Americans forced the pilot of a little Cessna sight-seeing plane from Miami to Cuba in 1962. Castro, apparently believing them to be CIA agents, forcibly packed them off on a foreign commercial flight to Miami. The two men were brought to trial in Florida and sentenced to twenty years for air piracy.

From 1963 to 1968 there were nine skyjackings from the United States to Cuba, five of them unsuccessful. Then in 1968 eighteen planes were successfully diverted to Cuba. The public became alarmed—to say nothing of the airlines themselves, who were plagued by nightmares of what effect a skyjacking disaster might have on them.

As political discontent in the United States became more radical in the late sixties, each skyjacking was an added embarrassment to a government deeply divided by dissent. Having refused to negotiate a skyjacking treaty with Castro in 1961, the United States had left him no choice but to grant American skyjackers political asylum, and the Bay of Pigs fiasco put him in no mood to help the United States out of its difficulties once skyjacking became a serious problem.

The thirty-five successful skyjackings to Cuba in 1969 produced a lot of shouting from all quarters but very little action to solve the problem. For every suggestion for prevention there was usually an objection from the airlines. The very thought of searching passengers or using security guards gave them fits. In 1969 the cures all seemed worse than the disease.

Eastern, one of the most popular airlines with skyjackers, worked with the FAA in developing a "psychological profile" of skyjackers and a metal detection system for passengers which was widely publicized and credited with decreasing the number of Eastern's instant charters to Cuba. The "profile" is classified material and like a lot of classified material lately, not a very well kept secret. In any case, I could serve no useful purpose by revealing this information here. The profile was arrived at without benefit of even one interview with a skyjacker, and although it might apply to a significant percentage of skyjackers, it also sweeps a good many *million* innocent air travelers into its net. Not surprisingly, harried gate and ticket agents have not been overzealous in its application.

The other airlines simply made sure all their pilots

were equipped with charts of Havana's airport and with Spanish-English language cards, while they continued to study the problem with an increasing sense of frustration. The trouble was, no one had any exact idea who the enemy was.

Then, on November 9, 1969, an odd thing happened. A group of six American skyjackers voluntarily returned from Cuba to face stiff prison terms and possibly the death penalty. Government authorities, delighted with this catch, hoped that publicizing the disenchantment of these men with Cuba would deter potential skyjackers. But the evidence that began to surface from examinations and testimony was perplexing.

It became clear that the skyjackers' return hardly signified a moral victory for the United States and democracy over Castro's brand of Communism. In fact, political convictions seemed to have nothing to do with the actions of these men. All things considered, the skyjacker revealed himself as a genuine screwball. The U.S. began to suspect something the Cubans must have known for ten years—that severely disturbed United States citizens were traveling to Cuba in stolen airplanes at great risk to many lives to seek mental rather than political asylum.

Far from being integrated into the Communist society, the skyjackers in Cuba constitute an expensive headache for the Cuban authorities.[3] And very little the Cubans do seems to please the black militant skyjackers (the only group to have called a press conference to complain about Cuban hospitality). There are two places in Havana called Hijacker House—one for American and one for Latin American skyjackers. "If my mother could see me now," an American skyjacker told a Canadian journalist. "I am living in a mansion with a swimming pool, a cook and gardener. The only trouble is that the cook and gardener are our guards, the swimming pool is empty and cracked, the house isn't kept up and is falling apart." She added that when the American skyjacker is considered too suspicious to live in Hijacker House, as many of them are, he is kept in solitary confinement in jail. The inmates of Hijacker House know of two suicides among them, and there is no telling how many have managed to do away with themselves in jail.

It is questionable what any country gains from severing diplomatic relations, but hardships incurred by both the U.S. and Cuba can clearly be seen in the case of skyjacking. The continuing hostility makes it impossible for either country to take steps to stop this dangerous game which nobody wins. Despite this, if Castro really wanted to call it quits and send our skyjackers back, he could easily accomplish this through intermediary diplomatic channels.

Actually, it amazes me that Castro has blinded himself for so long about the dubious gains of harboring our skyjackers. He is accepting and supporting our criminals—a significant number of them have committed crimes including murder before their skyjackings—as well as our crazies. He repeatedly runs the risk of an air disaster for which he will have to accept the responsibility, and if it happens over Cuban territory it poses a threat to his own citizens. These seem expensive and potentially tragic risks to take for the small reward of creating a nuisance for the United States government.

On the other hand, just suppose the U.S. government *really* wants to defuse the skyjacking threat and makes a sincere effort to re-open diplomatic channels. And just suppose that Cuba really turns her back and adamantly refuses to respond. Is it necessary to have Castro's cooperation to solve the problem? At this point, with governments and skyjackers all acting in a bizarre fashion, perhaps a bizarre solution might be in order. Why fight any country that harbors skyjackers? Let's *encourage* them.

Take Cuba, for instance. Many skyjackers still divert planes to Havana at considerable danger to the passengers and crews, because we have made skyjacking illegal. Couldn't the U.S. government defuse and even exploit the situation by encouraging our criminals if not our crazies *to* skyjack? ("You will be pardoned if you will remove yourself from the United States by skyjacking to Cuba and promise not to come back.") We might even consider flying whole prison populations to Havana. How many prison riots have touched off demands from the inmates for safe passage out of the U.S.? Let them go *before* they explode. It could save the government millions of dollars wasted each year on the brutalization of criminals and the dehumanization of the insane—more money than the cost of the diverted flights.

Unofficial intermediate stops in Havana could even be worked into selected southbound flight schedules. That way those passengers yearning to be skyjacked would be assured of a non-routine business trip to Miami. The skyjackers wouldn't have to use any weapons to convince the crews of their determination, so it really *would* be a joy ride. A lot of people might go for it—except, perhaps, Castro.

Of course, Castro might begin to get the idea that he was being used. He might even get mad and close the sanctuary. Imagine this quandary: by this time, the United States is benefiting so much from skyjacking—prisons, even mental hospitals, having been reduced to manageable populations—that we try to persuade Castro to keep his doors open by offering to buy his sugar, or extending foreign aid. At any rate, mission impossible accomplished.

Well, this is just my kind of *realpolitik*. As such it reminds me that the ability to write books has never been a certification of sanity. But then, on the other hand, neither has election to public office.

In reading the existing literature on skyjacking, along with the reams of distorted and incomplete information available from newspapers, I am continually struck by at least one consistent message—*all* political and legal systems seem unable to cope in any meaningful way with this particular pathological offspring of society.

The most obvious way to end the skyjacking era would be to return the skyjacker to the country of departure *immediately*. There is just no point in skyjacking a plane if there's no sanctuary at the end of the flight. Yet for many years governments have allowed themselves the luxury of double-think—skyjackers coming from a hostile nation were potential refugees; skyjackers departing their own country were criminals.

Sponsored by the International Civil Aviation Organization, seventy-seven nations from the Communist and non-Communist world met at The Hague in December of 1970 and drafted a convention which provided, among other things, that countries must *either* extradite the skyjacker *or* prosecute him under their own skyjacking laws. Because seventy-one of the participating nations signed the convention and eleven nations have ratified it, this agreement has been heralded as a major breakthrough in solving the skyjacking problem.

While it is heartwarming to learn that seventy-one nations can agree on *anything,* I just can't see that the Hague Convention does much more than make the skyjacking stakes higher by incorporating a possible prison sentence into the principle of political asylum. Politically motivated skyjackers are risking their lives to escape from regimes they consider to be oppressive, so what's a short prison sentence at the end of the line in the country of their choice? As for the crazy skyjacker, he doesn't seem to care about the consequences so long as he can escape across a hostile border. Thus the same political football game seems to be encouraged and condoned by the very institutions which claim to be trying to outlaw the sport.

It is interesting to remember public reaction to the Palestinian skyjackings, especially those of September, 1970, *and* to the foiled skyjacking plot of the Russian Jews who received harsh sentences under Russian law during the same period. The general reaction in the Western world was moral outrage at the Palestinians' political blackmail, and great sympathy for the plight of the Russian Jews. But what kind of sentences might those Russian Jews have received if they had been successful in skyjacking the plane to the West? How harshly would Egypt, Lebanon, and Jordan have dealt with the Palestinian guerrillas if they had been bound by the Hague Convention? What kind of a deterrent would that be to potential skyjackers?

My point is that the Hague Convention can't stop skyjacking since it doesn't do away with political asylum or privileged sanctuary for skyjackers. It just makes the game a more serious one—which may well provoke the potential player to use more desperate and violent methods for winning.

The existing evidence of mental disorders in many skyjackers should make every country that continues to accept skyjackers suspicious of categorizing them unquestioningly as political refugees. Skyjacking has shown itself to be a mental virus as virulent as any contagious disease. When resorted to by presumably genuine political refugees from countries with closed borders, successful escapes by air carry the virus, via publicity, to people less mentally healthy than *they* are. While all countries will turn back at their borders known carriers of serious communicable diseases, they continue to welcome the carriers of the skyjacking virus, making quarentine and the development of a cure impossible.

It might make good sense to call skyjacking (as well as any violent or threatening behavior) an expression of sickness, namely "insanity." The term, however, has unfortunate legal connotations, and certification of a criminal's insanity removes him from the ultimate jurisdiction of the courts. Since the U.S. judicial system is set up to punish rather than rehabilitate, the system satisfies some people's desire for vengeance but accomplishes very little else. A lot of people feel frustrated and cheated when *any* criminal offender is pronounced "insane." I'm not sure why—in most instances, indefinite confinement in an inadequately staffed mental hospital is actually a much worse punishment than a limited prison term.

It would be interesting to find out what society might learn about itself if all crimes involving the threat of injury or death to innocent victims were legally defined as "insane" and the offenders indefinitely confined to adequate, maximum security mental institutions for treatment. Although I have had very limited contact with criminals, those I interviewed were horrified at the suggestion that their behavior might be considered insane, and claimed that they would rather serve a prison sentence any day than be confined to a mental institution. But our legal system amply relieves such fears with punishment and parole, so most criminals can go out and pay back society with yet another violent expression of their frustration or madness.

Because successful skyjackings almost always involve the governments of more than one country, heads of state or their representatives at ICAO might assert their authority—before legal machinery even enters the picture—by accepting a new definition of the skyjacker as neither a political refugee to be protected nor a criminal to be punished, but a carrier and victim of a dangerous mental virus. They could then in good conscience return the skyjacker to his country of departure for medical and legal disposition. The word would get out that the game is over; the sanctuary closed. Not even a genuine lunatic wants to be considered crazy—it robs him of what he considers to be the rational reason for committing his crime.

I can hear the objections already: the political skyjackers from the Iron Curtain countries were not crazy, the Palestinians were not crazy, the Cubans who skyjacked to the United States were not crazy. And some will claim that the Black Panthers who have skyjacked to Cuba were justified in ripping off a free ride. Maybe so, but maybe that is beside the point. Defining skyjacking as a newly recognized and dangerous mental disease which respects no political border or legal system *from this point on* is at least as expedient as the political-refugee/criminal double-think. And *this* definition makes the negotiation of international treaties for the return of the skyjacker possible.

I would like to submit that committing the act of skyjacking makes a man a lunatic even as committing the act of murder makes a man a murderer. If it were known that skyjacking from here on is an unacceptable way to travel *for any reason whatsoever,* and that anyone committing this act will be judged mentally incompetent and returned immediately to his country of departure for an indeterminate term in a mental institution, those unfortunate people yearning to break through closed borders will be served notice to pick a less contagious means of escape. As for those sad, troubled souls who yearn to get away from themselves, let them seek the mental asylum they need by ground transportation.

2

EVEN IF one grants that the majority of *apprehended* skyjackers can be characterized as deranged people who seek mental asylum in Cuba, any discussion of skyjacking falls into muddy waters when the subject of the political skyjacker comes up.[1] The Palestinians offer the most striking example, since the present measures to deter skyjacking were a direct response to these multiple skyjackings in September, 1970. At that time the world witnessed the most bizarre series of crimes-as-political-protest ever dreamed up outside of the pages of science fiction. Four commercial aircraft were skyjacked by a small, highly organized group of fanatical Palestinian guerrillas [2] with no resources other than airplane tickets, unsophisticated weapons, and the suicidal/homicidal conviction that life is a cheap enough price to pay for bargaining power in the marketplace of world politics.

This scruffy, ill-equipped band of men and women not only succeeded in forcing three jetliners down on a desert airstrip with over four hundred passengers and crew members as hostages, but dealt some psychological and economic blows to the Western world which will not soon be forgotten. As the Jordanian army looked on helplessly from their tanks, and television cameras recorded the events for the incredulous eyes of the viewing public, the most glamorous technological symbols of our age appeared to be a less viable means of transportation than the camels wandering around them. Airlines and insurance companies heard the sickening sound of fifty million dollars' worth of airplanes being blown up in a demonstration of the newest form of power politics. Finally, governments broke their own laws to bargain for the lives of the hostages by releasing convicted terrorists and murderers. Minutely recorded for posterity was a multimedia documentary of governments being pushed to the brink of a multinational nervous breakdown.

Few will dispute the fact that the news media not only report current events but often help determine the course of future events. Every group with a cause must be painfully aware of the old maxim "out of sight, out of mind." It simply can't be denied that threatening lives and property in a spectacular manner like skyjacking insures front-page, prime-time coverage of the act and attention to the cause.

The Palestinian use of skyjacking in their terrorist activities against the Israelis was hardly new. On July 23, 1968, five members of the Popular Front for the Liberation of Palestine (PFLP) had skyjacked an El Al Boeing 707 to Algeria.[3] The crew and some of the Israeli passengers were held as hostages until September 1, when Israel agreed to release sixteen Arabs from its prisons, thus establishing the precedent of exchanging prisoners for hostages between the combatants. Once the Palestinians realized how vulnerable commercial aviation was to terrorist attack, public outcry against this behavior only made it a more attractive battlefield. Twenty years of being treated with cynical indifference by the major world powers had apparently produced an equally cynical disregard in the Palestinians for any socially acceptable method of conducting a war.

When a political group resorts to terrorism, revolutionary leaders dedicated to activism run the risk of losing control of the more criminally inclined members of the group. Such political groups often become an umbrella for apolitical followers who promote terrorist activities as a means of discharging their personal feelings of rage. This pattern can clearly be seen in the Palestinian war of terror on commercial aviation of the pro-Israeli world.

On December 26, 1968, members of the PFLP launched their first external attack on an El Al 707 leaving Athens International Airport by spraying it with machine-gun fire and incendiary grenades, killing one passenger, injuring others, and damaging the airplane. Israel retaliated by sending troops in helicopters to the international airport in Beirut, Lebanon, the city where the two Palestinian terrorists had been living before going to Athens. With cold-blooded efficiency the commandoes blew up thirteen Arab aircraft without injuring anyone or damaging any non-Arab airplanes. The magnitude of this economic reprisal was staggering. While the world was condemning Israel's overreaction to the PFLP attacks, this new and dangerous precedent was being incorporated into the terrorist's tactical manual.

On August 29, 1969, the PFLP combined skyjacking with economic terrorism. A TWA 707 was forced to fly to Damascus, Syria, by the now famous Laila Khaled and a companion PFLP commando. They added the Israeli touch, although not quite so successfully, by blowing up the nose of the airplane, causing $750,000 worth of damage. The practice of exchanging hostages for prisoners was again reinforced when a complicated agreement was finally reached in the first weeks of the following December, providing for the release of the Israeli passengers in exchange for a larger number of Arab prisoners—seventy-one in all.

Throughout 1969 and 1970 the PFLP continued to involve the Western world in its war with Israel by airport attacks and attempted skyjackings. The viciousness that characterized these attacks reached a bloodcurdling extreme on January 21, 1970, when a Swissair flight bound for Israel exploded at fourteen thousand feet, killing forty-seven people. On the same day an Austrian Airlines plane had a similar explosion but managed an emergency landing. Members of a Palestinian splinter group from the PFLP proudly announced responsibility for these acts.

The senseless murder and destruction, however, shocked even the Arab world. The high command of the Palestinian guerrilla organizations began disclaiming all prior knowledge of the terrorists' plans and joined the worldwide expressions of revulsion at such "inhuman" acts. It was not difficult for the Palestinians to grasp that their image had become monstrous in the eyes of the world. Still, commercial aviation as a battlefield had proved to be by far the most effective means of focusing attention on the Palestinian cause. The guerrillas had misjudged the methods and probably the homicidal insanity of some of their members.

During the spring of 1970 the Palestinians restrained their airline terrorists and consequently were pretty much ignored. While a great deal of attention was being paid to developing methods of dealing with skyjacking and airport security, little concern was expressed about the appalling refugee situation that had inspired the Palestinian acts of terrorism. The major powers were too busy pressuring the Middle East combatants to bring about a cease-fire.

In July the PFLP made the headlines once again, this time skyjacking an Olympic airliner to Cairo and holding the plane and passengers until Greece agreed to free seven PFLP terrorists serving terms for former attacks, which had resulted in two fatalities. As a minor operation it proved to the Palestinians that they could force other countries besides Israel to exchange prisoners for hostages.

Next, all the lessons learned in the past two years, both negative and positive, were synthesized by the PFLP in launching the audacious maneuvers that riveted all eyes on a small airstrip in the Jordanian desert.

On Sunday, September 6, four teams of PFLP commandoes boarded four flights—TWA Flight 741 in Frankfort, Pan Am Flight 93 in Amsterdam, Swissair Flight 100 in Zurich, and El Al Flight 219 in Amsterdam—thereby setting in motion a plan that had been conceived the previous July by the PFLP "revolution council."

A certain amount of improvisation seems to have characterized the project from the very beginning. Two of the skyjacking teams traveling on Senegalese passports and assigned to take over the El Al jet were refused seats when El Al officials became suspicious of them. Frustrated but not foiled, they booked themselves on a Pan Am 747 leaving for New York. An El Al official even went so far as to belatedly warn Pan American that they had two suspicious characters among their passengers on Flight 93 which had already left the gate for take-off. The nature of the suspicion was not elaborated on. Since he was not at all sure of what he was looking for Captain John Priddy personally searched the two men but found nothing. Reports are contradictory as to whether they had their weapons hidden in their undershorts or beneath adjoining seat cushions. Forty-five minutes later, Captain Priddy found himself looking down the barrel of the gun he had failed to uncover.

Under the circumstances it was a stroke of good fortune both for these skyjackers and for the passengers on the El Al flight that they were prevented from meeting the rest of their skyjacking team; otherwise the violent story that follows might have been a major catastrophe. The El Al officials were apparently lulled into a false sense of security by the decision to bump the suspicious Senegalese off the flight. There was not a glimmer of recognition as veteran skyjacker Laila Khaled (wearing a wig) and a companion boarded El Al Flight 219 bound for New York, despite the fact that Miss Khaled's picture had been widely circulated in the press and among El Al personnel after she had skyjacked the TWA flight to Damascus the year before.

When her companion made his move to gain entrance to the cockpit, he met resistance from the steward and one of the security guards, and a dangerous gunfight broke out. When the smoke cleared, the steward lay seriously wounded and the skyjacker was dead, but not before he had pulled the pin from a grenade which mercifully proved to be a dud. Passengers grappled with Miss Khaled and subdued her before she could activate the two grenades she had carried on board in her brassiere. The plane made an emergency landing in London to get medical attention for the steward, although El Al orders were to proceed to Tel Aviv with the captured Miss Khaled. When she was led off the plane in the custody of the British police, she defiantly proclaimed, "I will soon be free." She was right.[4]

Meanwhile the TWA and Swissair flights were headed for Jordan, following two bloodless coups by their respective skyjackers. The Pan American 747 proceeded to Cairo after picking up PFLP guerrilla munitions experts in Beirut. At the same time the world was reeling from the shock of this news, a PFLP member was lighting the fuse of his explosives aboard the Pan Am 747 while it was still two hundred feet off the ground over Cairo. The crew managed to evacuate the passengers safely and then run themselves as far as the wing tip before the first charge exploded. In a matter of minutes the 25-million-dollar airplane was nothing more than an insurance claim.

To the amazement of everyone except the PFLP the skyjacked TWA and Swissair flights were not headed to an international airport but to an abandoned World War II desert airstrip called Dawson's Field, twenty-five miles northwest of Amman, Jordan. Guided only by Jeep headlights and flaming oil drums, both planes—renamed *Gaza One* and *Haifa One* by the PFLP—landed on "Revolution Airstrip" forty minutes apart.

The 314 passengers and crew members then began the agonizing ordeal of waiting. They couldn't have been very reassured the next morning when daylight revealed the planes to be surrounded by guerrilla military and camping equipment, which was in turn surrounded by the much more impressive hardware of the Jordanian army. While governments were trying to establish communications with the guerrillas through diplomatic clearance, the passengers' passports were being examined by the guerrillas. Later that afternoon, Monday, September 7, 127 non-Jewish women and children were released and taken to hotels in Amman—a mixed blessing, since fierce street fighting had broken out in the faction-torn city, and its hotels were periodically caught in the crossfire.

Official condemnations of these outrages poured in from all quarters, but the guerrillas held steadfastly to their demands for the release of Laila Khaled and the PFLP terrorists imprisoned in Switzerland, West Germany, and Israel. Once the PFLP realized that England was reluctant to break her own laws and trade Miss

Khaled for hostages from other nations, a BOAC VC 10 with 115 passengers aboard was skyjacked on its flight from Bahrain and lined up with the other two stranded jets in the sweltering desert. One PFLP spokesman was quoted as saying, "There's plenty of room here for more."

The fighting between the Royal Jordanian forces and the Palestinian guerrillas expanded into a major civil war and complicated the negotiations for the hostages still more. Increasingly nervous about rumors of threatened military intervention from Israel or the United States, the PFLP evacuated all the passengers from the planes on Saturday, September 12, taking some to Amman and others, mostly American Jews and crew members, to unknown guerrilla hideouts. For the predictable coup de grace, all three planes were reduced to rubble by explosives.

In the anxious days that followed, some hostages were rescued by the Jordanian army while fighting swept over the hideouts where they were being held. But it wasn't until September 29 that the last of the hostages were delivered to officials of the International Red Cross. On September 30 Laila Khaled was flown in a British Royal Air Force plane to West Germany and Switzerland, where the plane picked up six more Palestinians and then flew on to Cairo. After twenty-four days the drama drew to a close. The last act was not so successful as the guerrillas had planned—no Palestinian prisoners in Israel had been part of the hostage exchange. But with the increasing difficulty of providing food and security to the hostages in the midst of the fighting, the PFLP seemed relieved to be rid of them.

In retrospect, the political gains from these skyjackings seem largely negative. The Palestinians briefly unproved their Neilsen ratings, but if anything, their plight is now worse since the Arab governments nervously keep them under surveillance at least, and the Jordanians are even systematically executing the most militant elements as fast as they can round them up. Certainly the world is more aware of the Palestinian cause, but those people who sympathize with them are no more able to do anything about it than protesters are to stop the Vietnam War.

There are other lessons, however, to be learned from this episode. With the advent of the "skyjacking group" the Palestinians have effectively served the world notice that nettlesome political or social problems can no longer be contained within a prescribed area and forgotten. Commercial aviation gives such groups a unique opportunity to draw the world's attention. An editorial in the *Berkeley Tribe* at the time of the skyjackings clearly stated the implications of the Palestinian success: "We are all the new barbarians. We are closer to the Palestinians than some would like to admit. We are the people without power in the world. Maybe soon, planes carrying very prominent international pigs like [Reagan] will be hijacked from the U.S. to parts unknown by, say, freaks."

The speed with which such an idea can spread is illustrated by an item in *The New York Times,* a little over a month after the Palestinian skyjackings: "Minneapolis. . . . A bold plan to kidnap Gov. Harold LeVander of Minnesota, hijack an airplane and use hostages to free Angela Davis and other prisoners was broken up by the police and Federal Bureau of Investigation agents today. . . ."

There is no reason to be complacent because such skyjacking groups have not yet emerged. It would be prudent to remember that the Palestinians trained and planned many months before they perfected their methods and that their experience is already incorporated in international guerrilla manuals. The Minneapolis group blew it, but to conclude from this that all revolutionaries are stupid is about as realistic as believing that all world leaders are wise, compassionate, and honest. If they were, redressing misery, ignorance, and social inequities would take precedence over war, profit, and power. And there might be fewer desperate men in the world motivated to skyjack.

3

"I SHOULDN'T TELL YOU THIS, but the 'unwritten directive' is to shoot the hostess if the skyjacker is using her as a shield, and that's the only way to get to him."

I offer this quote from a sky marshal just to show you the kind of information that sticks in my mind. I should add that I have been made the recipient of this unsolicited confidence *only* three times. Actually, it isn't the possible threat to my life that bothers me so much as the enthusiasm those three sky marshals seemed to have for the idea—my impression was that they would *rather* shoot a hostess than a skyjacker.

My real opposition to sky marshals, however, is based on a much deeper bias that existed before I had any contact with them. The past record of armed guards on airplanes is an alarming one. The Communist governments were the first to use armed guards as a counterforce against the threat of skyjacking, and this policy led to the loss of lives as well as airplanes. While it might have convinced their potential skyjackers for all too short intervals that skyjacking was unhealthy, sporadic skyjackings from Eastern Europe and Cuba over the past decade indicate that armed guards did not solve their problem but created worse ones.

The rest of us seem to have learned nothing from their experience—that although armed guards *may* have discouraged some skyjackings, confrontations between skyjackers and guards *certainly* have led to fatalities and crashes. Perhaps these totalitarian regimes felt it was worth that price to preserve their national prestige at the time, but the appearance of at least the Eastern European countries at the conference tables to work on international skyjacking agreements suggests that they are now considering that the price may be too high.

The sky marshal program proposed by President Nixon in October, 1970, was one part of the United States governmental response to the threat of skyjacking groups in general and to the Palestinian skyjackings in particular. The other part of this "deterrence program" was the widespread installation of metal detectors in airports and the introduction of passenger and baggage searches.

These preventive measures, which had been rejected over the years as commercially damaging or as potentially more dangerous than the crime itself, were hastily adopted amid elaborate rationalizations. Congress appropriated funds, and the airlines budgeted hundreds of thousands of dollars to support the program. The public breathed a sigh of relief: Uncle Sam was at last taking steps to protect them in the sky. A lot of us who work on airplanes can't help feeling that what these steps actually provided was a false sense of security, bought at great expense of taxpayers' and airlines' dollars.

Since the sky marshal program was created in response to the Palestinian skyjacking group, one might sensibly wonder about the skyjacking group's response to the sky marshal. Supporters of the program point to the El Al flight on which the skyjacking was thwarted by an armed guard with the help of the passengers. But that incident should be examined in the light of the Palestinians' intention to use four, not two, skyjackers on the flight.

The fact that the two Senegalese made the El Al official suspicious by purchasing two one-way tickets with cash—which is why they were denied seats on the flight—is common knowledge not only to us but to potential skyjacking groups as well.[1] Laila Khaled and her companion were fanatical enough to carry out their mission without the rest of the team. The PFLP had never encountered armed guards before, and underestimating the threat of force proved to be a fatal error on their part.

Their behavior suggests either that they didn't expect guards to be on the flight or that they were unusually suicidal. When the armed guard came forward from the rear of the plane and saw the steward struggling with the male skyjacker, he opened fire, killing the skyjacker and accidentally wounding the steward.[2] Miss Khaled was subdued by a passenger when she lost her balance as the captain put the plane into a steep dive. During the struggle she dropped her grenades before she could take out the pins.

It is horribly clear what would have happened had the pins been removed. But what would have been the outcome had the two Senegalese skyjackers also boarded the flight? Since all El Al crews are trained to act as soldiers in such a crisis—the captain refused to open the armored cockpit door; the steward heroically tried to disarm the male skyjacker; the armed guard risked killing the steward while firing at the skyjacker—El Al has made it clear that they are as determined not to be skyjacked as any Palestinian might be to skyjack, even at the possible cost of lives.

El Al certainly seems to have had the support of the passengers in this determination, as is evidenced by the behavior of the man who disarmed Miss Khaled.

"I'll blow the plane up!" she threatened.

"Okay, then we'll both die," he replied, and fortunately won the struggle.

One can assume that the intended addition of two more skyjackers to that flight would have all but guaranteed a tragic ending to the drama—armed guards notwithstanding.

The use of counterforce against airline terrorism, it should be noted, is supported by the Israelis and by many Zionists around the world. The Palestinians and the Israelis are at war, and war presumably justifies certain sacrifices, including the risk of losing airplanes and passengers' lives.

There is a certain consistency in the Israeli position which is lacking in the United States reponse to the threat of skyjacking. Most major United States airlines now carry sky marshals, but the crew members on those same flights are instructed to comply with the skyjacker's wishes in order to insure the safety of the passengers, who very likely feel no dedication to combat terrorism at the risk of their lives. United States crews are not drilled to react like soldiers; in fact, their entire training is geared to preserve lives, and until we are combat trained that includes skyjackers' lives, under *all* emergency conditions.

If potential skyjacking groups have learned their lessons from the Palestinian skyjackings, they could easily outnumber the sky marshals and disarm them or shoot them down as they reveal themselves. I have mentioned this possibility to many sky marshals, whose responses vary from admission of their relatively impotent position ("I'm no hero, better to be skyjacked") to an incredible faith in their guns and in the system ("We have 'information.' One time when Interpol informed us an attempt was going to be made, there were eighteen sky marshals on one flight.").

This last remark inspires a nightmare of a plane filled only with sky marshals and skyjackers, evenly matched: as they pick each other off—shooting through the cabin crew, of course—the plane explodes in a James Bond type of holocaust.

Phantasmagoria, to be sure, but not so farfetched as you might think.

And I ask myself, what is the point of it all? So far as skyjackers and sky marshals are concerned, confrontations between them can only prove to us what we already know: that bullets can kill and given certain conditions, that planes can fall out of the sky. I can't think what else could be gained by the exercise. Each group would claim victory and blame the tragedy on the other. Such are the results of blind dedication to the use of force and counterforce. Perhaps the outcome would also demonstrate to both sides that planes are unsuitable battlegrounds, but do we need a real tragedy to teach us that lesson?

In defense of most of the sky marshals I have talked to, they also are aware of the ambiguity of their position. There are so many conditions that must be met before they may act that as one sky marshal put it, "The way I see things, the skyjacker would have to be floating on the ceiling before I'm allowed to take a shot at him."

How scrupulously each sky marshal would observe such restraints in an actual skyjacking has so far been tested only once. On October 25, 1971, a skyjacker diverted a 747 to Cuba with three sky marshals on board. The sky marshals decided not to act because a hostess was being used as a hostage. As he deplaned in Havana, the skyjacker revealed that he had accomplished his feat with a ball-point pen and a comb wrapped in a sweater. The sky marshals, already angry at having been duped in such a manner, predictably were made the brunt of tiresome jokes. This is unfortunate, because such humiliation could inspire in some sky marshals a dangerous determination not to be bluffed another time. And a sweater-covered weapon could turn out to shoot real bullets.

Having talked to over fifty sky marshals, I was glad to learn that a number of them doubted that they would ever use their guns *first*. The majority, however, felt that they would try to prevent a skyjacking if they thought they could accomplish this without hurting anyone else. With few exceptions, all expressed the fervent hope that their theoretical reactions would not be tested by reality.

I wouldn't call the sky marshal's job an enviable one. Presumably the attractions of the job include travel to exotic places and independent work free from supervision and, possibly, carrying a gun legally, as is evidenced by the frequency with which sky marshals come up to hostesses and whisper, "Would you like to see my gun?" But then there is the exhaustion of flying thousands of miles with hardly enough time at the layover station to get adequate sleep, let alone enjoy sightseeing or shopping; long, boring hours of vigilance while other passengers drink, watch movies, and snooze; extended periods spent away from home. Sky marshals keep themselves awake by telling passengers their cover stories,[3] talking to hostesses, and playing solitaire. More than one of them has asked me to mention in this book that they have to fly too many hours at a time to remain really alert. Knowing my own early morning exhaustion after flying all night, I recognize the symptoms they describe—light-headedness and sluggish, clumsy physical reactions. And crew members fly only two thirds of the hours that sky marshals fly.

Along with heightening the possibility of a violent confrontation between skyjackers and sky marshals, the advent of the sky marshal may have cost skyjacked passengers their previous immunity from violence. In June, 1971, the first American passenger was killed by a skyjacker. This particular skyjacking demonstrates *all* the weaknesses of the United States deterrence program. The skyjacker bypassed the ticket counter (so much for the psychological profile) and the magnetometer (so much for the search) and rushed onto the airplane. He grabbed the stewardess as a hostage and ordered the passengers to deplane. When one man turned back to get his coat, the skyjacker panicked and pumped the passenger full of bullets, apparently believing he had gotten rid of the sky marshal (the flight carried none).

One month later, a man who had read about this skyjacking improved on the skyjacker's tactic in flight by ordering all the male passengers to remove their jackets and proceed to the front of the plane. No sky marshal was on this flight either, but after being apprehended, the skyjacker boasted that he could easily have handled one in this manner. Since the government has been publicizing some *female* sky marshals recently hired, we could soon be in for the longest skyjacking in history—while a prudent skyjacker flushes out the sky marshal by examining the contents of all the female passengers' handbags. (Promoting such a search as a necessary ingredient of a successful skyjacking might prove to be the first effective psychological deterrent for skyjackers.)

It isn't at all amusing, of course, to consider that passengers are losing their immunity from violence—a possibility the flying public seems blissfully unaware of. Their ignorance may explain why some passengers harbor a secret desire to be skyjacked: "I have to go to Miami tomorrow on a business trip. Every time I take that trip, I always sort of wish the plane would be skyjacked." I have heard such a longing expressed so many times that I've stopped counting. As one federal aviation official put it, "It sure takes the blahs out of air travel." [4]

It's pointless to condemn this attitude. Up to now most skyjackings have largely provided an unexpected thrill for the unharmed passengers, who could look forward to being a local celebrity on the cocktail circuit. It beats talking about that business trip to Miami any day. Just listen to what one woman who had been *terrorized* with her children during the September, 1970, Palestinian skyjackings had to say: "We couldn't have bought a trip like this, seeing all the things we've seen, right, kids?"

I don't want to give the impression that all passengers want to be skyjacked. The patience and good humor with which they endure magnetometer and ground marshal searches before they board their flights suggest that the majority of them want to help avoid any unexpected side trips. At the end of these searches the crews are likely to end up with a rag-taggle collection of concealed and unconcealed weapons to be returned to passengers at the end of the flight: pen knives, scissors, gun cigarette lighters, African souvenir spears. One young cowboy had to relinquish his cap pistols and holster set. Some passengers find these searches reassuring. One man told me, "You people give much more thorough searches than the airline I came down to New York on. Makes me feel you care more." Of course, we care, sir, but do you really think those searches affect the number of skyjackings?

I don't. But I heartily approve of searches anyway—at least they discourage passengers from trying to bring concealed weapons on the airplane. And it's surprising how many people carry them. As of January, 1972, over three hundred and fifty passengers had been arrested for trying to board an aircraft with firearms. And an astonishing number of guns and switchblades had been found abandoned in airport washrooms and potted plants after their owners discovered they would be searched before boarding the plane.

But so far as discouraging skyjackers is concerned, the effectiveness of these searches is questionable at best. I know of one instance when a gun was found on a very distraught and impecunious young man who confessed to being homesick for Lebanon. It is possible that he might have attempted to skyjack the plane had he been allowed to board. But then consider the skyjacker mentioned earlier who bypassed the magnetometer and search and shot a passenger, or the one who used a ball-point pen and comb.

In discussing the effectiveness of searches there is no avoiding a very touchy subject. Most ground marshals are understandably reluctant to search the areas of the body where smart skyjackers might be likely to hide their weapons. Laila Khaled, among others, is now famous for wearing grenades in her bra. In July, 1971, a skyjacker tipped off the mechanism of the magnetometer, was *not* thoroughly searched, and accomplished the first part of his skyjacking with a gun hidden either in the genital area or, possibly, underneath his belt. (He was searched by a harried gate agent, not a ground marshal with the authority to conduct a thorough search.)

So long as skyjackers continue to hide guns and grenades in these areas, and ground marshals and gate agents continue to observe the niceties by failing to search them there, skyjackers will continue to board airplanes with concealed and dangerous weapons.[5]

I can't think of any happy solution to this problem. On a trip to South America three years ago I was searched before I left Rio by a lady guard who struck me as overly enthusiastic about her work. Unprepared for the search in the first place, I found the experience humiliating. I'll admit that I didn't know the facts about skyjackers' tricks at the time, but then the average airline passenger today is as ignorant of these facts as I was. Imagine the uproar of indignation if genital searches became standard procedure. Passenger patience and good humor would be a thing of the past. And from the hostess's viewpoint facing a planeload of passengers who have just been sexually offended by a thorough body search is a nightmare.

The fact is, skyjackers don't have to resort to hiding guns in their bras or shorts. If crazy and determined enough, they can find ample weapons on board the airplane. And consider how many skyjackings have been accomplished with the threat of nonexistent weapons. In addition to the ball-point pen and comb gambit, there is the skyjacker with a history of mental illness who diverted a flight all the way to the Bahamas by threatening to set off the explosives tied around his waist—which turned out to be rolls of mint candy. Another example, and there are many, is the skyjacker who used a "bomb" concealed in a handkerchief to divert a flight to Havana. When the Cuban guards uncovered the weapon, they found a bottle of Old Spice shaving lotion.

In pointing out how often skyjackers have made a mockery of the current efforts to control them, I do not mean to imply that we are completely at their mercy. I do feel that the present emphasis of the United States goverment's deterrence program is misguided, ineffective, and possibly dangerous; and that there *are* constructive steps that could be taken which have so far been ignored.

Granting that the most obvious solution to the majority of skyjackings is denying sanctuary to skyjackers, it is also obvious that neither the United States nor any other government can accomplish this miracle of cooperation single-handedly. But the Congress of the United States has made the working out of bilateral or multilateral agreements all but impossible by defining skyjacking as a crime punishable by *death* or life imprisonment. Until the death clause is removed from that law, many countries that find the death sentence for this crime abhorrent—for example, Italy and Cuba—will refuse to sign any extradition treaty for the crime of skyjacking. I'll admit that these particular countries' objections to the death sentence hardly reflect a morally superior attitude—Italy doesn't have a skyjacking problem yet, and Castro isn't so indulgent about Cuban citizens stealing planes. But officially our death sentence clause prevents the working out of treaties with other countries besides these two, so it would seem more realistic to try to change the United States law than to try to change other countries' objections to it.

An added disquieting thought is that emphasizing the death penalty (there are now signs all over every airport and at the entrance to every commercial airplane) has already made some skyjackers realize that they have nothing more to lose by adding homicide to the crime of skyjacking—proving at best that the threat of death is effectively deterring only those people who wouldn't dream of skyjacking in the first place.

The Federal Aviation Agency has spent a great deal of time and effort studying the problem of skyjacking. They have worked with the airlines for over ten years devising the various deterrent measures now in effect. Yet in those ten years not one person responsible for helping develop the deterrence system has examined even one of the people he is trying to deter. Nor has any crew member officially been given any information on what is known about skyjackers or about the ways some crew members have safely thwarted skyjackings.

Whenever there is an airplane crash, the airlines and responsible federal agencies examine meticulously every piece of machinery and debris, question intensively any crew member involved, to discover the cause and prevent a repetition of the accident. It would seem that we are much more clear-sighted about investigating the causes of mechanical than human disasters. Isn't it possible that examining the people who have gone haywire on those same "machines" might help us avoid a disaster of the same or greater magnitude?

The thought has occurred to the FAA, but the President and the United States Congress gave the FAA the job of solving the skyjacking problem without giving them the privilege of examining the cause of the problem—namely, the skyjacker. Psychiatric examinations of the many skyjackers in our federal prisons and mental hospitals would shed invaluable light on their motives for committing this crime, and with that knowledge some effective means of managing a skyjacking once it is in progress might be devised. But as things stand now, one FAA official describes skyjacking as "a drama in which all the actors are amateurs."

From what little is already known about skyjackers' motivations and their reactions to crew members, there is every indication that the crews could easily improve their performances at least to a semiprofessional level. It is unrealistic to expect crew members to become psychologists, but instructing them as to sensible and safe behavior when confronted with irrational, possibly dangerous people in the air would surely reduce the panic level and even prevent a lot of unnecessarily successful skyjackings.

You might think that once this oversight was pointed out, something would be done to remedy the situation. The snag here is that once the skyjacker is apprehended he comes under the jurisdiction of the Department of Justice. If the Attorney General's office wanted to cooperate with the FAA in this venture, I have no doubt that skyjackers would be made available to the FAA or some qualified institution for examination. But although nowhere is it stated or admitted that skyjackers *cannot* be examined, every FAA attempt to set up examinations thus far has been strangled with bureaucratic red tape and unofficially voiced disapproval—which means, in reality, no examinations.

Questioning an official of the Justice Department about this situation, I first got the typical run-around reply: "That's not my department, permission for examinations would have to come from the Bureau of

Prisons." I asked him if endorsement of such a program from his office or, preferably, the Attorney General's office might not make the Bureau of Prisons very co-operative. (After all, we both knew that disapproval had been expressed to the FAA from some mysterious high office before the FAA even approached the Bureau of Prisons.) Highly irritated by this line of questioning, he came stunningly to the point. He declared that although there was evidence to define many criminals besides skyjackers as mentally unbalanced, those offenders were still being punished rather than *treated*—meaning, I gathered, that making an exception of skyjackers was out of the question. I had the impression that he thought I was a little crazy myself to suggest that one small category of bizarre criminals might make a suitable guinea pig for an experiment of enlightened legal and medical treatment, just to see if it would work.

My difficulty with this man, of course, was that he didn't understand the reasoning behind my questions at all. I shouldn't have been surprised—after all, he was a government official. The government, which can't see that in response to their sky marshals some skyjackers get violent, also can't see that in response to their magnetometers some skyjackers resort to nonmetallic explosives which won't register.

Even though the new weapons detection devices will be sensitive to all kinds of explosives, there will be a time lag because of expense before these devices can be installed at all airports. Once they're installed—assuming their fallible human operators make no mistakes—skyjackers will probably figure out new ways to get around them.

What if information obtained by examining skyjackers revealed that a much more effective deterrence program could be devised at a fraction of the cost of the present one? That, for example, sky marshals are a waste of money?

Given the unhappy choice, I'd rather face an unbalanced skyjacker with a gun in his hand any day than one with a homemade bomb who, like me, would have had no experience in handling explosives. As a hostess I would be a lot more willing to learn the best way to handle skyjackers than to learn how to handle explosives (even though there may be a better way to get rid of a hand grenade than throwing it down the lav).

Thoughts like these have apparently occurred to other crew members as well. The Air Line Pilots Association (ALPA, a union whose membership comprises pilots and cabin crew members from all over the country) has recently passed a resolution urging psychiatric examinations of skyjackers and the development of audiovisual aids to convey the information thus gained to all airline crews. Since unions can have very loud voices, the Attorney General's office seems to be listening at last. But at this point their cooperation is only a promise, and since the government has already taken ten years even to consider the advantages of psychiatric examinations, the pilots might be well advised to check the ALPA offices for bottles of Arpège.

As for the crew members themselves, I have to say that their former passivity in tackling the skyjacking problem has contributed as much as anything to the official feelings of helplessness and frustration that inspired the adoption of deterrence measures to control our own fears instead of the crime.

Until crew members organize to effectively protest their use as pawns in the political chess games that is skyjacking, we will continue to have unscheduled side trips to hostile countries with guns at our heads.

Maybe there are other offices where the loud voice of a union could be heard.

4

SKYJACKERS HAVE always struck me as more crazy than criminal. Performing such a public crime inside a closed environment like an airplane—with a seated audience literally captive—suggests to me that something more is going on than the illegal procurement of transportation from A to B. From my first days of interest in skyjackers it occurred to me that they might be frustrated, desperate people who saw airplanes as glamorous yet vulnerable symbols of power—also symbolizing a spectacular means of escape from their problems and a public forum for saying to society, "Look what you have driven me to do."

It also occurred to me that to someone who feels defeated by the world, who feels beaten down by repeated failures, skyjacking offers an opportunity to reverse the process. When a plane leaves the ground, it becomes an autonomous microcountry or political unit. While it is in the air, the captain is the king of the country, the crew his lieutenants, and the passengers his subjects, whose lives depend on his skill and their obedience to his orders. Simply by using a threat, the skyjacker brings about a coup d'état, putting himself in the position of authority and controlling the outside forces he feels have put him down all his life. He in fact becomes king, the passengers and his crew his fearful subjects.

I concocted this theory on no real evidence whatsoever, because there was no information available on skyjackers' motivations at that time. Nevertheless, I was quite carried away with it until I began to consider the millions of abject failures who don't fight their despair by taking over airplanes. On the other hand, skyjacking *has* become an increasingly popular way of acting out. What would happen if the trend continued? A waiting list of skyjackers for each flight? Surely not—there were all those faceless failures in my imagination saying, "Don't look at us, lady. We're afraid to fly."

I told my theory once to a psychiatrist who nodded with interest until I got to the part about the pilot being the king of a country. He corrected me: "You mean the *father*." I was a little irritated because I meant "king," considering not only the fact that any head of state has a lot more power than most daddies, but also the fact that the king could be a queen. And in any case I think power, not title, is what's at issue. What kind of pandemonium will we have if the pilot someday turns out to be a woman? A lot, if people like that psychiatrist continue to divide people into sexual camps.

But I wanted to ask him some questions and I spoke his language a lot better than he did mine, so we called the king "daddy." Unfortunately, even with this concession, he was unable to offer any clue as to why so many American skyjackers divert planes to Cuba—I couldn't believe that they were all dedicated Communists and revolutionaries. Consequently I was left with a theory full of holes, now translated into Freudian terms.

Then, in the summer of 1970 I came across an old issue of *Parade Magazine* that carried an interesting news item:

> Dr. David Hubbard of Dallas, Texas, a psychiatric consultant to the U.S. Medical Prison Center at Springfield, Mo., has interviewed twenty persons accused of hijacking. According to Dr. Hubbard, . . . "It is utterly untrue . . . that these men are left-wingers or Communists. Most of the hijackers I've interviewed are rightists, ultraconservatives, members of the radical right. . . . Basically," he explained, "hijackers are unhappy people who want to do away with themselves. They pick Cuba because they are convinced it's a land of no-return. They would just as soon choose any other country if they thought the barrier between that country and the U.S. was impenetrable. People who commit suicide frequently use it as a means of calling the world's attention to their unhappy state. Hijackers hijack planes with much of that same motivation."

One nice thing about working for an airline is that plane trips are slightly less expensive than long-winded long-distance phone calls, so I flew to Dallas to see Dr. Hubbard. If I thought I had a burning curiosity about the mysteries of skyjacking, Dr. Hubbard's was a conflagration of enthusiasm. Through many visits I played Dr. Watson to Dr. Hubbard's Sherlock Holmes.

His theory of skyjacker pathology had been developed—unlike mine—in an orthodox and respectable manner: first the evidence, then the theory. No one was more surprised than Dr. Hubbard when he examined two skyjackers in one day at the Federal Prison Hospital: "I thought I was hearing an echo when the second skyjacker came in and started using the same phraseology, describing the same dreams, giving the same sort of background." In his six years as a psychiatric consultant to the Prison Hospital he had in fact *never* come across two men committing the same type of unusual crime with such astonishingly similar psychic makeups. He began to wonder if further examinations of individual skyjackers might lead him to constructive knowledge about skyjackers in general. After an arduous search for interviewable skyjackers which took him to remote prisons all over the United States, he was able to find twenty subjects. His examinations of them gave him enough material to draw some tentative conclusions about a general skyjacker pathology which in his opinion indeed sets them apart from other criminals. He published these initial findings in a book, *The Skyjacker: His Flight to Fantasy*, and continued to interview every available skyjacker, the total amounting to forty as of this writing. The additional interviews did not significantly change any of his previous conclusions.

Although the first set of twenty skyjackers comprised the politically unaware and ultraconservatives, Dr. Hubbard told me then that someday he was sure to run across a solidly left-wing skyjacker whose motivations to skyjack would derive from the same personality failures exhibited by the apoliticals and right-wingers. His prediction came true a few months ago when he interviewed a skyjacker who had been active in liberal and left-wing causes since adolescence. The skyjacking attempt, labeled in the press as engineered by a black militant organization, was thwarted when members of the organization reported to the police that one of their people had freaked out and was planning to skyjack. In an interview with Dr. Hubbard the skyjacker bitterly described the personal failures that had led to his being ostracized from the militant group, and the frustration and depression leading up to the futile attempt to escape from these failures. As seemed the case with all the skyjackers who talked to Dr. Hubbard, politics really didn't have anything to do with this one's motive for skyjacking.

Dr. Hubbard and the psychiatrists who have worked with him on assessing these psychological factors that unite the skyjackers interviewed all agree that such similarities cannot be coincidental. From the evidence gathered in these interviews they have been able to put together a composite picture of the skyjacker's psychological makeup, which makes the act of skyjacking a little more understandable:

As a child the skyjacker is slow in learning to walk and, later, clumsy and unsure of his physical coordination. Many skyjackers' first memories precede walking, indicating not an unusually acute memory but a below-average motor ability. Some did not walk with any facility until they were three or four years old.

The skyjacker's earliest and most persistent dream memory is a terrifying nightmare of paralysis. "Something was after me. My body was heavy, heavy, heavy." "I couldn't get away." "I was all slow motion, my hands and feet were made of lead." Coupled with his lack of physical coordination, the nightmares of paralysis have a disturbing threat of reality to him.

The frustration resulting from the dreams and the clumsiness often resurfaces in adult dreams of being able to fly (those who had such dreams flapped their arms when describing them) and an obsessive interest in sky-diving, flying lessons, and the manned space flights. One skyjacker even claimed to have mastered "astro-travel" in his waking hours. All he had to do was think himself across the ocean: "Last night I visited a certain place in India, near New Delhi . . ."

Dr. Hubbard feels that a revealing clue to the skyjacker's motivation can be found in his description of the family structure, which in most cases boils down to a violent, often alcoholic father and a zealously religious mother who came to represent two opposing forces. In terms of emotional allegiance the child is confronted with a wall of hostility between the two parents. The mother woos him with virtue; the father subdues him with violence. The child soon learns that he can jump the hostile border between the two parents. If he angers his mother, he can hide behind his violent father, who uses this defection to try to taunt the mother out of her virtuous passivity. If his father lashes out at him in an alcoholic rage, his mother provides emotional asylum and comfort. "Skyjackers have been turncoats from the time they were three years old," Dr. Hubbard said. "It's no surprise that their adult crime should involve crossing an actual hostile border between nations."

By the time the skyjacker is five he has been won over to his mother's side because the emotional support she offers is more constant. The more he strengthens that alliance, the more his father rejects him. In his identification with his mother, who looks to heaven for her support, the skyjacker learns to respond to aggression and violence with the same passivity, the same masochistic endurance of abuse. ("At home we prayed a lot and often talked about hell and what would get us there; all kinds of little things were dangerous. . . . Heaven sounded pretty good." "Almost anything can send a person to hell, like losing your temper or picking your nose.")

In this emulation of his mother the skyjacker becomes the victim of bullies at school and, often, the prey of either sexually precocious older girls or older homosexually inclined boys. The mother's early emotional support turns more and more into emotional demands as he grows into adolescence. Often he has a little sister whose social protection is made his responsibility, thus limiting even more his opportunities to escape this female domination in play with boys his own age. In explaining his failure to make friends or participate in sports, one skyjacker commented with resignation, "Besides, Mother and my sisters sort of had me on their team."

So far, circumstances and his reaction to them have robbed him of his masculine identification. He is clumsy, passive, and lonely—totally lacking in self-confidence and self-respect. Victimized by the violence of his father, the emotional demands of his mother, and the cruelty of aggressive children who spot him as a patsy a mile away, the skyjacker was programmed for failure by the time he was five.

As the perennial fall guy he has no way to release

his anger. The skyjacker's prototype for the expression of anger is his father, who works over the family and the furniture at the slightest provocation, real or imagined. But his mother puts a taboo on any overt expression of anger, telling him he won't get into heaven if he follows his father's example. Although there is plenty in the skyjacker's life to make him angry, the only acceptable way for him to deal with anger is to swallow it, which produces emotional indigestion and depression—resulting, predictably, in the skyjacker's becoming the target of his own rage.

The skyjacker leaves home; he may join the army, believing that such a positive action will allow him to escape from it all. The catch is that he takes with him his own self-image, shattered years ago in childhood. Although he has the appearance of a grown man, possibly even a tall, muscular man, he sees himself as a weak, cringing misfit—too shy to ask a girl out, always the victim of those more clever, more confident than he is.

Having developed a seemingly limitless capacity for losing, he has no tolerance now for winning. Even if he is fortunate enough to meet people who encourage him to value himself, he manages to put impossible demands on himself, exaggerating every mistake he makes, canceling out any realistic self-appraisal. He accuses himself of being miserably inadequate and unmanly. He has already become his own deadly enemy.

The lifetime of anger boiling inside of him becomes increasingly uncontrollable, often taking the form of paranoia. It manifests itself in mocking voices in his ears, torturing him with hateful reminders of his pathetic state. Or he may cast his superiors or even perfect strangers in the role of persecutors who are out to get him. More than one skyjacker described how "people" had wired his car with explosives or poisoned his food. A unique expression of self-hatred was exhibited by a skyjacker who was certain he had skin cancer and insisted to a number of doctors that his skin "stank." Convinced that only the devil's territory—by which he meant a Communist country—could cure his affliction, he applied for a visa to Russia. When the Russians were understandably reluctant to provide him with one, he decided that Cuba would do and skyjacked. After being apprehended—and, presumably, at last suitably punished for his sexual sins (he had lived with a woman he'd met in a mental hospital without the sanction of marriage)—the skyjacker claimed that his affliction had been miraculously cured by a bowl of soup served by the warden of Dade County Jail.

If the skyjacker becomes sexually involved with a woman, she is usually the aggressor. He still does not go out with girls—"I didn't know how to ask"—and sex carries with it the freight of guilt from childhood when it was associated with the hostility between his father and mother. The image of his father (the devil) violating his mother (the saint) inhibits his own sexual performance, very often rendering him impotent or at best extremely passive. His profound belief in his inability to do anything right as a man provokes the women in his life to ridicule him, reinforcing his pattern of failure. His passivity, of course, makes him a lightning rod for other people's antagonism and abuse.

The skyjacker's fantasies about being free of his

miserable self-image offer him the only respite from this intolerable situation. Very often the fantasies involve actual flight and delusions of grandeur. He envies the astronauts; he dreams of being an airline pilot. His response to emotional stress, in fact, is to "go away" from it literally. He uses cars and commercial airline flights to put space between him and his problems. Often very long distances are involved—pointless round trips by air two and three times a month (when one skyjacker's wife told him she was leaving him, he rented a car in a fit of rage and drove from Houston to Los Angeles to Colorado and back to Houston three times in three weeks). This sort of activity alternates with physical inertia—long hours spent escaping from reality in front of a television set or sitting alone brooding.

Very early in his studies of these skyjackers Dr. Hubbard began to notice evidence of vestibular disturbances. The inner ear, the vestibulum, is the organ that controls the body's equilibrium. If its function is sufficiently impaired, no balance can be maintained at all. If the disturbance is mild, the person will feel a little unsteady but with effort can still stabilize his body posture. Consider the temporary swaying motion most people experience immediately after they step off a boat: a normal inner ear will quickly adjust to the steady gravitational force on land, restoring the body's equilibrium. But one skyjacker who had returned from Cuba by sea continued to react to the sway of the ship for a week after he had been on land.

Late walking, poor coordination, feelings of heaviness—all reflected in their nightmares of paralysis and earliest memories—indicate that the skyjacker's physical responses to gravity may have been scrambled from birth. This in turn could explain his obsession with motion and flight as attempts to overcome or at least temporarily stabilize his body's capricious relationship to the ground.

Since the vestibular organ is acutely sensitive to emotional as well as physical impact—"Sit down, I have some bad news for you"—the skyjacker's pursuit of motion during times of emotional stress may not be surprising. It would follow that if physical disequilibrium precedes emotional instability, the body's stabilizing mechanism—the inner ear—would first have to be soothed before the emotions could be brought under control. The skyjacker's compulsive drives and flights over vast distances and his dreams of flying thus take on added meaning.

This is bold theorizing on Dr. Hubbard's part, based only on secondary evidence, and he is the first to admit that the theory is not provable without extensive testing on the skyjackers' inner ears. It is also one of the most controversial points in his theory, because of the implications it could have about certain types of criminal behavior. The Justice Department is hostile to the very notion of possible—even partial—physical explanations for crimes. How can you legally indict an inner ear?

The Department of Neurology at Northwestern University Medical School is willing to make the complex vestibular tests on the skyjackers free of charge any time the Justice Department gives permission, which would prove or disprove this important part of Dr. Hubbard's theory once and for all. Until that permission is granted we are left with educated guesses as to the relationship between these vestibular disturbances and the skyjacker's crime.

As the skyjacker gets older, his behavior becomes more and more obviously disturbed, causing him to lose jobs, to move, or in one skyjacker's words to "crawl back" to his family. For ten offenders in Dr. Hubbard's original group of twenty skyjackers, unsuccessful encounters with the workaday world resulted in such extreme psychotic behavior that they were committed to or voluntarily entered mental institutions for varying periods of time. Five of them attempted suicide, whereas others with stronger religious prohibitions about taking their own lives fantasized situations in which someone else did the job for them.

Although four of the skyjackers had criminal records, their crimes were of a nonviolent nature, mainly petty theft and forgery. The majority had never seriously considered breaking the law before skyjacking. What, then, could inspire a meek man who had shunned violence and force all his life to suddenly, radically change his behavior and commit a spectacular crime? And why in the air?

At what Dr. Hubbard calls the terminal moment, everything converges on the skyjacker to nullify his very existence. Having used up his meager inner resources fighting previous failures, he now finds himself jobless, friendless, loveless, and hopeless. The voices in his ears are becoming more persistent. The fantasies of people out to get him turn his thoughts more and more to violence and revenge through murder, suicide, or rape.

His characteristic passivity is now being challenged by his near volcanic anger at his failures; the resulting inner struggle seems to be pulling him apart, threatening to reduce him to a state of infantile helplessness. He feels he must either change the direction of his life or be extinguished by these forces.

Remembering the vestibular disturbances, Dr. Hubbard thinks it is significant that the skyjackers all described this conflict and their ultimate solution to it—skyjacking—in terms of body image. Expressions like "down on my knees" and "they had me crawling" were repeatedly used to describe the psychological state leading up to the skyjacking. Their thoughts immediately prior to the act centered on the need to stand upright: "I had to stop being the sniveling little bastard that I was and stand up like a man." "Once a man has learned to stand and have dignity, you can't take that away from him." "It was my first stand-up."

Like an unsteady toddler in the grip of a murderous rage, the skyjacker is terrified of acting on his violent urges and equally terrified of *not* being able to. The nightmare of paralysis threatens to become a reality. The struggle to control these urges and hold himself together depletes what little strength he has, to the point that he instinctively realizes the next step in this regression is the infantile state—a nonperson totally imprisoned by the dreaded bonds of gravity.

In a last desperate attempt to reverse this downward spiral the skyjacker must cope with his physical disequilibrium before attempting to steady his emotional balance. He does this by affirming his ability to stand on his own two feet "like a man"—*in the air,* because flying has always symbolized freedom from the hostile force of gravity and his own scrambled responses to it.

In proving to himself that he can stand up like a man, he also takes the first step in abandoning his passive identification with his mother for a try at the tyrannical male role of his father. He then transfers his destructive urges to the crew of the aircraft. By threatening the stewardess with a gun, he commits what is probably his first aggressive sexual act against a female, revenging himself against all the females who have ridiculed his manhood. ("She jumped. It made me feel better that I could scare her.")

By taking command of the aircraft, he defeats his father—the captain—along with all the bullying males in his past. At the same time he effects an identification with the pilot, the man with wings on his chest, whose occupation he has always envied. He then directs the pilot to transport him across a hostile border in a replay of childhood defections from one parent to the other.

Cuba, the most common destination, represents a land of no return where he will be either killed or granted sanctuary; at the time of his act he doesn't have any real concept of the future. He has gambled everything to fly out of his private hell; if he can't escape his past, then he'd rather die, because, to him, he will at least die *as a man.* Even if his attempt fails to get him across a hostile border, he has achieved his own kind of psychic victory by substituting a crime in which he could act out all his violent drives symbolically for the *actual* crime of suicide, murder, or rape. In that moment he has simultaneously defied the laws of the land and of gravity, while staying within the laws of heaven. In that moment, ever so briefly, he has been master of himself.

His act ensures a highly dramatic production for everyone involved. But the starring role is played by that stumbling misfit, the skyjacker. Not all of Dr. Hubbard's subjects turned in Academy Award performances. Although four of them were convincing enough to divert planes to Cuba, the majority ran into a cast of characters who refused to cooperate once they realized the skyjacker was more suicidal and confused than homicidal and determined.

Dr. Hubbard found no appreciable psychological differences between those skyjackers who succeeded and those who were taken directly into custody in the United States. All were curiously docile and detached after their act. Having actually rendered their lives more meaningless than ever, they all seemed peacefully resigned to the fact that their future was now someone else's responsibility. ("I had no great desire to go to Cuba. I think I pretty much fell into a position where everything would be taken out of my hands and solved for me.") Having purged themselves of their most destructive urges, they reverted to their previous moral, nonviolent roles, sometimes even expressing disapproval of skyjacking and bewilderment about their own participation in the crime.

The conviction that the skyjacking had prevented them from committing a more reprehensible crime is one of the most common reasons used by the offenders to explain—but not excuse—their actions. One skyjacker who had been obsessed with the idea of raping his daughter before he fled to Cuba listened to Dr. Hubbard's description of the psychological effect of rape and incest on little girls, thanked him, and said, "If that could have been the result on my daughter, then this whole damned thing was worthwhile."

Another offender, who had already served his prison sentence when interviewed by Dr. Hubbard, became a lay preacher for the Jehovah's Witnesses. When Dr. Hubbard mentioned the apparent contradiction between the crime he had committed and his new religious dedication, the skyjacker said, "Don't you see, there is no middle country for me. I must be on one side or the other of the issue of violence. If I weren't a preacher, what sort of violence might I do?"

Although no longer actively suicidal, many still admitted to a preoccupation with death as a release from their troubled lives. The four who succeeded in getting to Cuba voluntarily returned to the United States to face the death penalty, which suggests at least a passive interest in dying. One skyjacker with strong religious convictions sadly concluded his interview with Dr. Hubbard by saying, "I am an individual placed on this earth for but a short time, in order to do those things that will give glory to God. Yet I fail because the world snatched me from the monastery, in which I had been destined to remain. This was my chance at happiness. . . . My country had abandoned me. I pray that God has not done so, for what is left? I long for the day when

I shall hear the words, 'Come, my love, my dove, my beautiful one, the winter is over and the rains have ended.' "

The act of skyjacking becomes a little more comprehensible within the crazy framework described by Dr. Hubbard. So far it is just a theory—based on some very real psychological evidence—but to quote Dr. Karl Menninger, "To have a theory, even a false one, is better than to attribute events to pure chance. Chance explanations leave us in the dark; a theory will lead to confirmation or rejection."

With all due respect to Dr. Hubbard—and I have a great deal—I have to admit I have one real problem with his theory. Everything fits very neatly when you consider the skyjacker a "he" (as "he" is referred to throughout). But what about the female skyjacker? Were Laila Khaled and the other women skyjackers "standing on their own two feet" and proving their manhood? Things get a little touchy here, because maybe they were.

In answering this troublesome question, Dr. Hubbard described all but one woman skyjacker in the pure Freudian terms of sexual confusion or denial—"really masculine broads"—reducing their actions to overcompensating for their secondary sexual status, i.e., no penis. Whereas he views the male skyjacker's quest for manhood with a certain compassion, I definitely got the impression that he, like most psychiatrists, finds women to be dreary interlopers, messing up good theories. ("What does woman want?" lamented Freud.) The one female skyjacker who gained Dr. Hubbard's sympathy and a modicum of respect was spared his contempt, perhaps because she was terribly fragile and feminine-looking and shared her skyjacking with her boyfriend whose "manhood" she was trying to help him prove, although, in Dr. Hubbard's words, "*she* had the balls."

Freud's brilliant foundation for modern psychology certainly still serves to explain much of man's behavior, but I become more and more convinced that those theories within Freud's original narrow context of "man's" behavior not only explain but also perpetuate an artificial and crippling set of values based on sex. How long will it be before we stop equating penis with power and power with being right? Before we start teaching people to think of themselves in terms of their heads instead of their genitals?

That women as well as men can become so confused about what is valuable in themselves that they act out some perverse psychodrama to attain a dubiously exalted ideal called "manhood" tells me a lot more about society's standards than it does about individual behavior. That some pathetic man can derive an unconscious sexual thrill from sticking a gun in a hostess's stomach tells me a lot more about the status of women in general than it does about the offender's relationships with the females in his life. That a psychiatrist can explain the acts of all these sick people to me and not question the arcane psychological premises that reinforce the division of men and women according to sex roles; that he can fail to hear the contempt in his own voice when he describes a woman skyjacker, pathetically trying to imitate *his* male standards, as "a really masculine broad"—only explains to me why this whole screwy setup is going to continue for a long, long time.

During my conversations with Dr. Hubbard, I would inevitably come up with other questions for which there were no easy answers. One particularly disturbing one was, "What would these men and women have done if they hadn't skyjacked?" The depressing answer? "They probably would have committed suicide, murder, or rape," or, almost as depressing, "They would have given in to the paralyzing regression that was driving them back to an infantile state and ended up just another inmate in our overcrowded mental institutions."

It is appalling to think that despite the ever increasing knowledge of aberrant behavior amassed by researchers, we are still unable to devise any effective means of identifying and aiding these unhappy people before they put themselves outside the bounds of society. We have intricate military early-warning systems, but the possibility of a psychic early-warning system is largely just a dream. As society itself takes on more of the aspects of a madhouse in which we are all inmates, depersonalized and shoved from one ward to another, what hope is there of a cure for the ravaging disease of generalized inhumanity? All I have to do is take a ride on the New York subway to realize how many of the people surrounding me seem to be on the verge of going berserk. At best, I can realistically pray that one of them doesn't short-circuit his last connection with reality until after I reach my stop.

I avoid attacks of alarm brought on my fellow inmates of the underground simply by choosing surface transportation. But I can't help imagining that if something isn't done about skyjacking, airline passengers may start regarding each other in that same light and opt for boats or trains. Is there no alternative vehicle to offer these people who seem compelled to quest for their "manhood" in the sky?

A resourceful fellow from the National Institute of Mental Health once proposed the establishment of an organization called Dial Skyjack, providing the same advisory function that suicide prevention agencies have found to be so effective. Well, why not? S-K-Y-J-A-C-K even has the right amount of letters for a telephone number. Of course, a telephone call is not a trip, no matter what Ma Bell claims.

Well, the government has had to discontinue a daily airlift to and from Cuba, at least partly because of the dearth of Cuba-bound passengers. Why not reinstate this airlift and call it Skyjack Airways? The plane could carry medical personnel, dressed as crew members and ready to play their proper roles in the psychodrama and help the skyjacker through his/her "terminal moment." Since he would not have committed a crime by revealing himself in this way, the skyjacker could then be treated medically rather than disposed of legally. A publicity campaign could inform potential skyjackers that they now have their very own airline, encouraging them to dial S-K-Y-J-A-C-K and make a reservation.

A mad solution to an insane problem, but it has its own internal logic. It would give the news media a legitimate angle for informing the public about skyjacker pathology; there could even be television commercials:

"Fly Skyjack Airways, the wings of people who want to get away from it all." Of course, it's not just mad; it wouldn't work. A skyjacker wants to take command, not be given it. And what potential skyjacker would even consider some little airline that had the effrontery to call itself Skyjack Airways? I can just hear them saying, "They must be crazy and probably don't even know how to fly."

The only other proposal I can offer is that the National Institute of Mental Health subsidize the commercial airlines for providing a therapeutic theater for skyjackers until an effective solution to the problem is found.

As I said before, the subject of skyjacking unravels the lunatic fringes decorating all our psyches. I am no exception.

Theories about human behavior have a certain neatness—even elegance—that the actual behavior of individual humans seldom has. ("But Doctor, I swear I'm not in love with my mother. It may be true that the woman I married is exactly like her and is making my life miserable, but that has nothing to do with my *mother*.") As the average neurotic man struggling with an Oedipal complex hardly takes on the grandeur of Oedipus Rex, neither is the individual skyjacker perfectly typecast in the dramatic role of the "typical" skyjacker. While I have never heard of a real man who succeeded in marrying his mother, I do know of skyjackers who have not limited their acting out to *symbolic* crimes of suicide and murder. Some have committed murder before and during skyjacking, and others have committed suicide after. And who knows about the unreported rapes?

As a recent phenomenon skyjacking gives every indication of erratically mutating with society's response to it. To me, society's alarming display of machismo (sky marshals, for one) is as sick and sickening as the skyjacker's pathetic quest for it. If publicizing security measures is indeed increasing the potential for violence in skyjackings, it's not the first time the communications media (with some help from the airlines) has unwittingly aggravated the skyjacking problem. For sheer stimulation to the point of levitation, what could be more provocative than most television airline commercials? They all seduce us with promises to take us away from it all. The precise aim of every airline advertising campaign is to stir up fantasies in fairly stable people to go right out and jump on a flight to some exotic place, leaving their mundane, tiresome problems behind. And here comes the skyjacker on the evening news: sensational! *He* took those commercials literally and made off with an airplane. In a momentary identification with the skyjacker a lot of law-abiding upstanding citizens, sipping drinks in front of television, think a little enviously, "I wouldn't have the guts to do that," and assume that the skyjacker—criminal or not—must have a lot of courage.

"There's a little bit of the skyjacker in all of us," admits Dr. Hubbard. This is why, despite all the obvious evidence that skyjacking is a crazy and dangerous crime, it also has a crazy appeal to the public.

Despite the unarguable connection between publicity and the perpetration of spectacular crimes, press censorship wouldn't really solve the skyjacking problem at this point (although more responsible reporting would surely help). Skyjackings seem to occur in cycles—after a lull, news of one will usually touch off a whole series. Oddly enough, the chronological record shows that unsuccessful skyjackings have stimulated new cycles almost as often as successful ones. And each new twist added to the crime (and loudly heralded by the news media) inspires imitators—*every* time. Just how many skyjackings would occur in the absence of the added stimulation of sensational publicity will remain an unknown unless the press voluntarily censors itself. But, unfortunately, by now the possibility of skyjacking is firmly entrenched in the mass consciousness anyway.

I do wonder what effect expanded and more balanced news coverage would have on potential skyjackers. Would there be the same willingness to identify and inspiration to emulate if, in the process of reporting any skyjacking news, the pathology of the offender were stressed? Emphasis on cowardice, failure—perhaps even that blow below the belt, sexual inadequacy—might rob the skyjacker image of its machismo.

Gathering evidence and information to develop a theory of skyjacker pathology is a pointless exercise unless some constructive use can be made of the knowledge gained. The marked suicidal tendencies in skyjackers, as well as diplomatic considerations, would indicate that the death penalty should be abolished. And from another view, despite the "promise" of the death penalty, we have yet to implement it. Having met all too many people who find this discrepancy deplorable, I think it would be more humane and *safe* for all concerned to remove the invitation to execution and inform everyone that skyjacking is not a passport to heaven or any other carefree paradise.

Crazy as some of the skyjackers are—and some are a lot crazier than others—every one interviewed by Dr. Hubbard admitted that he wouldn't have considered skyjacking had he known that immediate extradition for mental appraisal and legal disposition would follow. In itself, this is a convincing argument for using the denial of sanctuary to deter the potential skyjacker.

Suitably enlightened by Dr. Hubbard's theory, I still wondered how a real skyjacker would conform to these generalizations. Since most of them are in Cuba or in prisons and mental hospitals, an available skyjacker is a pretty rare bird. I was finally able to flush out four of them: Gladys and George, Sam, and Raffaele. Although in many ways they fit the skyjacker pathology, I have to admit that they are also another story, as you will see.

Except in the case of Raffaele Miniciello, whose name and exploits are too well known to disguise, I have not identified any skyjacker in the chapters that follow by his or her real name. I doubt that this will accomplish anything more than my heeding my own warning about publicizing criminals. Since many skyjackers have already admitted that personal notoriety was at least an added incentive to commit the crime, I decline this opportunity to contribute even in an insignificant way to such satisfactions.

Maybe Andy Warhol's suggestion that everyone in the world be allowed five minutes on television to be a celebrity *would* cut the crime rate. It might even make television more interesting.

5

White sneakers outside
  the music room door
    tells me your home

The creak of moist satin
  on hardwood floor
    tells me your home

Blue smock-hiked up
  ballets up and down
    tells me your home

flannel blue
safety-pinned
bedtime you
makes me grin

How I love you

—*George's notebook*

How do you describe a couple of kids who sky-jacked? It begins with a love story, but not one Erich

Segal's readers would appreciate. The girl was Gladys, sensitive and fragile-looking, at nineteen a promising flutist and ballet dancer. Her boyfriend, George, was an intelligent, peace-loving college student of twenty-one. Armed with a kitchen knife and a can of insect repellant, the two of them attempted to skyjack a Miami-bound flight to Cuba in the beginning of 1969. They were apprehended in Miami after the pilot convinced George that the plane needed to refuel. The court gave them an indeterminate sentence, and they were paroled after serving two years in federal prisons.

A picture taken at the time of their arrest shows Gladys looking no more than fourteen, her downcast eyes and delicate mouth framed by Alice in Wonderland hair. George's childlike face is adorned with a moustache, and his black hair touches his shoulders. Looking at the picture, you can't help wondering what lay behind those innocent eyes to make them desperate enough to attempt a skyjacking—and with such unlikely weapons.

Gladys grew up in a medium-size city in the East, the second of two children. Her childhood was characterized by conflicts between her parents over her father's drinking and the resulting job problems. Although both parents had college degrees, Gladys's mother, with an M.A. in music, was the one who was steadily employed, giving private piano lessons. Gladys's father often became violent when drunk and was particularly hard on her older brother. Cruel as this behavior must have seemed to his son, it was perhaps less damaging than his manipulation of Gladys. The father initiated a near-incestuous relationship with her when she was four, which continued until she was thirteen. At that time he proposed actual intercourse. She finally confided in her mother, who threw the father out and obtained a legal separation from him.

As Gladys grew older, the atmosphere of secrecy surrounding her relationship with her father made her suspect that their behavior was abnormal. Feelings of guilt over this secret caused her to avoid the company of children her own age. During this time her mother was periodically under psychiatric care for minor nervous disorders brought on by the strain of her role in this bizarre household. Her husband all but ignored her, offering sexual attention to his daughter and violence to his son. By the time the mother threw the father out and attempted to pull the family together, Gladys was already severely emotionally damaged.

Gladys remembers getting high on pills before she could force herself to walk to school. At the age of thirteen she was raped while in a drugged daze on the way to class. After that, she used sex with several boys in a pathetic attempt to establish a close relationship. "I know this is corny, but I really wanted somebody to love me, you know? I really did." Her feelings of guilt about sex made any meaningful attachment impossible.

At the age of fifteen Gladys sat down in the kitchen one afternoon and calmly swallowed enough Benzedrine, aspirin, and sleeping pills to end her confusion about it all. Discovered by her mother, she was rushed to the hospital where she remained in a coma for thirty hours. She was kept in the psychiatric ward for two months. After she left, psychiatric therapy helped her to sort things out enough to try living again.

Two years later, Gladys saw George leaning against a fence one summer evening and, she says, immediately fell in love. He was living with one of her girl friends at the time, but over a period of a few months the attraction between Gladys and George intensified while his problems with the girl friend increased. When the girl friend finally left him, George and Gladys began their love affair, which they both describe in terms both lyrical and cosmic. They became totally absorbed in each other—sharing everything, inventing their own language, writing reams of poetry.

George moved in with Gladys on the top floor of her mother's house. Gladys's mother liked George and was happy that her daughter had found someone to love her. Feeling these concerns to be more important than moral conventions, she warmly accepted George into the household.

George's background can't match Gladys's for sheer wanton abuse, but his upbringing was dominated by the conflict between an authoritarian, heavy-drinking father and a devout mother who brought him up according to strict Catholic principles. He attended parochial schools and obediently became an altar boy to please his mother. Since his studies were mastered easily, he spent most of his spare time playing basketball and baseball. It wasn't until he started high school that his parents began to consider him a problem. George started flunking courses, left the church, and, like many of his generation, rejected the demands of a competitive society while at the same time finding himself too confused and paralyzed to seek positive alternatives.

"I began to think about getting older and getting a

job and things like that, and I began to look at what was happening around me. I felt very depressed thinking about it. I used to ask myself what I was going to do and how I was going to live and I didn't have any answers. So I just pushed the whole thing off the desk—off my mind. I'd go out and run around and play basketball and drink quantities of beer." Later a friend introduced him to pot, and getting stoned became a more effective escape route.

George's father, who worked as a clerk in a large distributing firm, was embittered that all his efforts to advance to an executive level had met with failure. His frustrations were often released by drinking too much, which would inspire him to attack objects that symbolized the members of the family—he'd tear up his daughter's clothes or knock the refrigerator to the floor. He never subjected the family to physical violence, but George suspected he would have liked to but was too cowardly to act on these urges. His father's example depressed George, who felt sorry for him but was determined not to emulate him.

His father, feeling the distance between them, would try to enlist his son's support by telling him that the men had to stick together against women. George, however, remained more sympathetic to his mother, whom he felt didn't deserve such bullying. His mother, however, preferred his half-sister—four years older than George and the offspring of her previous marriage to a World War II casualty—and George largely remained an outsider in the family. He continued to accept financial support from them while muddling through high school and two years of a junior college.

When he was eighteen, George became seriously involved with a girl much more sophisticated than he. She had her own apartment, and after numerous battles with his parents over this relationship, George moved in with her. George felt ashamed that he was using this girl "as an escape action and as a kind of forward scout for my life. . . . She had gone on and set up a world of her own. She did all the dirty work, but I just kind of stepped into it."

When the girl began to show signs of depending on him too much, "wanting things like silverware," George provoked arguments which eventually drove her away from him. It was during this period that Gladys stepped into the picture. In her shy but determined way she kept coming around, just looking at him with her haunted eyes. George was intrigued but puzzled by Gladys, whom he considered aloof. She would mysteriously show up at odd hours and then disappear for a week or sometimes for a month. After the girl friend left, Gladys began coming around more often, and as they talked, her defenses slowly melted away. George was amazed to find himself deeply committed to her.

Having found the capacity to love another person, George began to worry about his ability to take care of Gladys. She gave him such great joy, he felt, that he ought to be a positive influence on her life. Instead, his aimlessness and confusion about the future seemed to be sapping her own ambitions. She had given up her dancing after he expressed his disapproval of the strenuous bar exercises. (He confessed later that he was actually jealous of the time she spent practicing.)

Neglecting her flute practice, she started spending all her time with him.

George began to have a fantasy. He could really make something of himself if only he could break free from all the things like cigarettes, Pepsi-Cola, and pizza which he felt chained him to the soft life. Reality intruded on this dream when he discovered he would soon be eligible for the draft—his scholastic average wasn't high enough for him to transfer to a four-year college. He mentioned Cuba in a half-serious way to Gladys, who immediately got very excited about the idea. They could go away together and work in the sugarcane fields and never be separated. The only way they could get there was to skyjack, and at Gladys's urging George began to make plans.

During her interview with Dr. Hubbard in prison, Gladys claimed that she was apolitical, although she believed George to be a radical. But she insisted that their decision to go to Cuba was not really based on politics. It was simply that "there didn't seem to be anyplace for us, there really didn't." Gladys also felt that the skyjacking itself was a chance for George to prove his virility. It was Gladys who provided the kitchen knife as George's weapon in addition to the can of insecticide. The same knife had been used by her brother to threaten her when they were children. "You see, to me it was like the coming of manhood for him. The first stand-up. Like, all the other time he was hiding."

With the triumph of optimistic expectations over anything approaching balanced judgment, the lovers packed their bathing suits and Gladys's flute and set off to catch their plane, figuratively and literally.

I went to see Gladys and George a month after they were released on parole. The taxi left me in front of a white clapboard house in a pleasant middle-class neighborhood. As I walked up to ring the bell, I felt apprehensive about the effect my intrusion might have on these two dreamers—paroled to the past after having failed to reach the point of no return.

Gladys answered the door; tiny and too thin, dressed in a long flower-sprigged dress. "Good, you're blonde," she announced in a high, breathy voice. "George likes blondes." She led me upstairs to George's room, cluttered with posters, magazine pictures, snapshots, drawings, love notes, books, records, a phonograph, and a little round table surrounded by three chairs where we could all sit and look at each other. On the table sat a rag doll on a cardboard throne, to whom I was ceremoniously introduced. The doll, with long black hair and moustache, looked familiar, and I suddenly realized that it was the image of the George whose picture I had seen at the time of the arrest. This George looked quite different. His hair was much shorter now, just curling down and around his ears, and the moustache was gone. I asked him why he had cut his hair.

"Just because you look like a freak doesn't mean you're a good guy anymore," he said. "Some freak with long hair and a beard came up to Gladys in the subway in New York. Turned out to be a masher." George grinned, and I noticed that one front tooth overlapped the other slightly, making his grin lopsided. I couldn't seem to shake off the feeling that I was in the playroom of two precocious children, politely tolerating an adult intruder. I reminded myself that George and Gladys were respectively twenty-three and twenty-one.

For lack of anything better to do I give them a copy of *Flying High,* my book about what it's like to be an airline stewardess. Feeling more than a little ridiculous under the circumstances, I relax somewhat when they both assure me that they are pleased with the gift. George further eases the tension by saying, "Hey, I've written a book, I'll give you a copy." He rummages in a box in the corner and extracts a yellow cardboard-bound collection of poems and stories which he has mimeographed. Having put me at ease, they offer me coffee and fig newtons—tea party in the doll's house.

I mention George's participation in Dr. Hubbard's research project on the skyjacker's inner ear. Dr. Hubbard is confident that his theory about the connection between vestibular disturbance and skyjacking will be proved, which would help the airlines and the government to save $225 million presently being spent on security guards.

"Big deal," George says. "I don't know why I should try and save the government $40 million. They'll just go out and buy bombs with it."

Gladys giggles and adds, "Now every time we do something wrong, we lurch around and blame it on our inner ears."

She suggests that we take a walk to the park. George, still thinking about the government buying bombs, doesn't respond. "You know I need to go to the park a lot, don't you?" she says quietly. George wakes up and smiles yes. While she is changing her clothes, George admits that he doesn't like to go out much; that he is more comfortable when surrounded by boundaries like four walls. When I ask him why, he shrugs.

"You know, general paranoia. I'm the kind of person, once I get comfortable with things, I like to hang on to them. Gladys is just the opposite, she has to get out of the house, I guess because of her mother and all that."

Walking downstairs, Gladys asks if we should take her mother, who lives on the ground floor.

"Mumsy is a beautiful person," George informs me.

Mumsy emerges from the shadows of an alcove off the music room, where she gives piano lessons—a short. middle-aged woman with a pixie face wreathed in smiles and framed by short graying hair that sticks out every which way. Her eyes look at me with friendly anxiety. After being assured that we really want her to come with us, and ascertaining that I am a Gemini, like her, she pulls on her boots, chattering away all the while about charting my horoscope.

It is nearly dark when we step outside. Winter bleakness, crusty snow, icy paths, and puddles that look frozen and then give way to splash us with muddy water make Mumsy wail: "I thought this was going to be a nice brisk walk to the park, you guys, and instead Ole Mumsy's gonna break her neck. Hey, hold on to me, I don't like this." George and Gladys hold up Mumsy as we slip and skid along. In the park George and Gladys race up a hill while Mumsy and I trudge slowly to the top. When we get there, they are already down the other side and swinging back and forth on some tiny tot swings. In the fading light their two immature figures don't look at all out of place in such a setting—swings, seesaws, slides. Trying to connect all this to skyjackings, trials, and prisons, I give up.

By now, Mumsy and I are freezing, and when she mentions Mr. Prince, who runs the ballet school where Gladys and Mumsy work, George suggests that we go and visit him. "He has a real Victorian house with real gaslights. Everything is authentic."

Mr. Prince's house is indeed a restored Victorian manse filled with antiques, gaslights, even a huge black iron stove. Mr. Prince comes into the kitchen, very much the ballet master; George and I immediately straighten up and snap to attention. Gladys and Mumsy are bouncing up and down, doing pliés; Mr. Prince picks up his cue and struts around, clapping out the rhythm with his hands. Tommy, a man who shares the house with Mr. Prince, comes downstairs from a nap and shuffles around making us drinks as he blinks the sleep out of his eyes. Suddenly he snaps awake, crushes Mumsy in a bear hug, and shouts in her face, "How old are you?" Mumsy collapses and giggles, while I wonder why.

Mumsy's conversation is characterized by a devastating spontaneity. Every thought that comes to mind tumbles out an instant later. She explains from the floor: "One night I woke up around two thirty, in the morning and found a strange man on my bed nuzzling me and feeling me up and down. I said, 'What do you think you're doing?' and he grabbed me by the shoulders and shouts, 'How old are you?' I told him I was forty-nine and he just went back to nuzzling me and saying, 'I just want to bite off a little piece.' He didn't rape me, so I guess I was the wrong age." Mumsy looked puzzled, as if trying to decide whether or not she had been insulted.

By now Mumsy is talking nonstop, while Mr. Prince sparkles with anecdotes about his travels with a well-known ballet troupe. Gladys and George are quiet and seem remote from the proceedings. Although I am enjoying myself, I began to have misgivings about ever accomplishing the purpose of my journey and wonder if perhaps that isn't the point of all the diversions. There we are, sitting in an antique parlor with the gaslight casting a soft glow over us, surrounded by relics of an age innocent of airplanes—a charming "let's pretend" atmosphere.

Mumsy and Tommy go into the hallway, and in the half light they slowly move out of sight as they climb the stairway, solemnly facing each other. In a few moments they reappear from another direction. I really think I have flipped out, until it is explained that they are playing with an elevator left by the former tenants, presumably infirm.

I welcome the suggestion that we all go out and eat: a Chinese restaurant, glaring light bouncing off white walls and whiter rice. Mr. Prince, Mumsy, and Tommy sit facing us—Mr. Prince still sparkling, Mumsy looking dazed but happy, Tommy asleep, dormouse fashion.

The subject of the skyjacking finally comes up when a friend of George and Gladys who knows about my book joins the table. "It's over and done with," George says quietly. "There's no point in going back over it again and again."

The next morning Gladys served George and me fried eggs on the little round table in their upstairs sitting room. When she told me she had been sick with colds and flu ever since she left prison, I offered her some vitamin C. Her expression as she looked at the tablets before putting them in her mouth made me feel she was trying to muster up the courage to take a handful of arsenic. It was a distressing sight, and I was on the verge of telling her to forget it—maybe it's less painful to have the flu—when she managed to swallow them.

"It's really hard for me because I swallowed a whole bottle of sleeping pills once," she explained matter-of-factly. "I washed them down with wine punch, and it made me feel so sick I kept being afraid I would throw them all up. Every time I take a pill now it makes me think of that."

She finished her coffee and ran off to help Mr. Prince block a ballet for a recital in the spring, leaving me with George. George sighed, as though resigned to his fate, and plunged into "the story," as he called it.

"Here I am hung up, I can't break out, I can't get away for whatever reasons. So how you gonna ever get out and get away from your mother and father. Ah, ha, now here's a thing in the newspaper that says these guys have hijacked an airplane. Now all these guys do is take a little pencil or something and go into the cockpit and tell the captain to fly to Cuba. And you don't have to be overtly violent, because the captain of the aircraft has such an awesome responsibility for the lives of all the people aboard that he more or less has to go along.

"This is marvelous. You can get on a plane, and four hours later you can be two thousand miles away from New York State, you can be in another country where you can't drag along all your Catholic school culture. Either you're going to have to kowtow to everybody in the country and become the little sniveling bastard that you are, or you're gonna have to get up on your two feet and become a man. You get in the corner of a sugarcane field and start chopping, right?" George was pacing around the room, his face agitated and serious.

"You make it from there. Tabula rasa, clean slate, right? That's the beauty of it?" He looked at me with questioning eyes and then sighed. "Only it doesn't work out that way.

"I wasn't prepared to do a lot of violent things, and when the captain of the aircraft saw that—kaput!" George brightened for a moment and said, "For five or ten minutes these guys are really flipped out." His smile faded. "But after that the shock value has worn off, I don't look so weird anymore. So the guys say, 'Why don't you sit down?' And it turns out we are in South Carolina and we've got an hour or two to go. I'm sitting there with my little thing and they're talking about religion and the guy comes back with the Our Father and I'm really flipped out now. No, no praying, I say." Remembering the scene, George rolled his eyes.

"I wasn't prepared to knick his ear with my knife

or set off my aerosol can, and they knew it. These were just token things. When the plane was coming down into Miami, I knew this was a bummer. I said, 'Oh, man, somebody's gotta do something, somebody's gotta do something,' over and over again, louder and louder. 'Cause this was it—twenty, thirty, forty, sixty years. 'What are you doing to me,' I said. 'You're talking all this Christ shit and here you're gonna crucify me.' I said, 'Why don't you just do the thing, it's not gonna kill you.' " George shuddered.

"Anyway, I had fifty dollars in my pocket and I gave it to the captain and told him to go back and give it to Gladys and get her the hell out of here. And then I heard her screaming my name, and I knew they had her and they had me. And that was that." A weak smile.

I asked if they had bought tickets to Miami. "Yeah, it was worth it, right?" At a loss for a response, I asked if it really was. "Yeah—you know, theoretically." He laughed. "It's better than eighteen years of therapy or whatever. It just seemed like *the answer.*" Emotions chased across George's face—elation, sadness, resignation, and, suddenly, indignation. "I think they took a big chance. How did they know I wouldn't blow up the plane? I was pretty freaked out." Looking at George's eyes I knew what the crew had seen—fear and confusion, false bravado perhaps, but more than anything his gentleness and the childlike innocence that allows him to believe in easy escapes. Certainly there was no trace of the craftiness or slyness that might convince a stranger that he believed the end justified the means. It occurred to me that if George had put a nylon stocking over his face, he might have made it to Cuba.

"It's not the biggest thing that ever happened in my life," he said defensively. Noticing my puzzled expression, he flushed and said, "Well, yeah, I guess it was pretty big. Just a day, though," and added softly, "just a day that lasted two years."

I asked him if he really thought he had resolved anything by skyjacking. "Oh, yeah, something had to be done. And I did something, for better or worse. And now the worst has happened. They've picked you up and put you in prison, which is what you were worried about all along. So what can they do *now?*"

On the train back to New York City I read George's notebook. One ironic little poem made me remember his description of almost missing the train the day they skyjacked. "We overslept because it was a really foggy, dark day," he had told me. "We had to grab our stuff and wake up Mumsy to drive us to the station. Made up some story to tell her 'cause we didn't want her involved and it really made us feel awful. When we got to the station, we ran out to the track and way down, and chugging away into the mist we could see this silver rear end of the train getting smaller and smaller. It was really far away and we started yelling and running after it. I thought, 'Jesus Christ, there goes my *life!*' And you know what? It stopped. And very slowly it started backing up to pick us up. It was really beautiful and eerie. You know, I was all keyed up to *do* it, and if that train had left without me, I just might have lost my nerve."

Flying Scared

The poem read:

Locomotives

And good reasons too
    Caused
    Our

Psychopaths
    To cross.

6

SAM THE SKYJACKER. A patriotic fellow who wanted to vindicate the honor of his country by assassinating Castro. Needless to say, his ambition was unrealistic, considering, among other things, his choice of weapon: a broken, unloaded gun, only slightly less lethal than Gladys and George's knife and aerosol bomb. But then, Sam's six-foot-four-inch muscular frame looked a lot more menacing than the two fragile hippies.

In January, 1969, Sam boarded a flight at Jacksonville, Florida, and forced it to Havana. After 109 days in solitary confinement in Cuba, he was put on a ship for Canada, where he turned himself in. A member of a Green Beret reserve unit in a Southern city, Sam suffered repeated head injuries during parachute jump practices with his unit. He pleaded temporary insanity at his trial. His lawyer claimed that he became confused after these head injuries to the point of a mental breakdown the night of the skyjacking; that he believed himself to be a member of a CIA-FBI plot to assassinate Fidel Castro. Two psychiatrists from the

Federal Prison Hospital at Springfield testified that in their expert opinion, Sam was indeed "temporarily insane" at the time of the skyjacking. The prosecution charged that Sam was just plain drunk and consequently responsible for his actions. After thirty minutes of deliberation, the jury decided that Sam was "innocent by reason of temporary insanity." This was the first acquittal of any skyjacker of a commercial airliner.

One of the psychiatrists whose testimony had helped acquit Sam was Dr. Hubbard. And Dr. Corbet Thigpen, an Atlanta psychiatrist who is best known as coauthor of *The Three Faces of Eve,* examined Sam and wrote in his deposition for the court that Sam ". . . probably had a paranoid character for years" and sees himself as ". . . a knight in shining armor who wishes to rescue the nation. . . ." Thigpen concluded: "I find nothing in him that was malicious. Even the motivation of this act was patriotism"—an opinion neither Castro nor the crew of the plane could be expected to agree with.

I wondered how Sam came to see himself as the "knight in shining armor." His early background reveals nothing extraordinary. Sam was born in one of Georgia's coastal cities, where his father still owns a profitable lumber and planing mill, built up through hard work since the Depression. For the past ten years he has worked for his father, who is a devout Lutheran. His mother is a Baptist, and both parents placed a great deal of emphasis on religious training during his childhood.

When Sam's little sister died at the age of six, Sam became especially close to his mother in an attempt to help make up for this loss. "It was like I just had to fill in my sister's shoes," he told the judge at his trial. His mother never really recovered physically or emotionally from the death of her daughter.

Sam went to the University of Georgia, where he concentrated more on basketball than on studies. He left after one quarter to return to Savannah and marry his high-school sweetheart. Married nineteen years, they have four children.

To me, the most inexplicable aspect of Sam's skyjacking was the active cooperation of his wife and a captain from his army reserve unit. First he persuaded his wife to drive him to the captain's house, *after* telling her about his mission to assassinate Castro; then he gave the same story to the captain, *who drove him to the airport.* In view of Sam's history of head injuries, which had produced periods of depression and peculiar emotional responses, I wondered how the two of them could have gone along with his fantasy.

Sam's wife, Carolyn, said in court that a month before the skyjacking a chain at the planing mill had swung loose, hitting Sam in the head and knocking him out. She described his behavior after that as withdrawn and erratically emotional. He brooded a lot, especially about the decline of American patriotism. He broke down and cried while watching a television interview with a girl from the South who had joined the revolution in Cuba and who claimed she would even kill Americans if they threatened invasion. His wife also testified that there were times when Sam didn't seem to recognize old customers or looked through her as though he didn't see her. This behavior had worried her—Sam is well known in Savannah for his high-spirited friendliness and especially for his courtly manners with women.

Informed by his lawyer that Sam would be happy to talk to me, I set off for Savannah. Carolyn had called and invited me to stay with them, the warmth of her Southern hospitality penetrating the frost of the New York Telephone Company. She assured me that in Savannah people knew how to make strangers feel welcome—even airline hostesses who want to interview skyjackers. I believed her.

The woman who met me at the airport was petite and blonde, her hair carefully arranged in a cluster of curls at the back of her head. Her six-year-old daughter, Jenny, slept on the back seat. Driving through Savannah out to the island where they live, we passed oak groves bearded with moss and sleepy rivers fanned by warm ocean breezes. Carolyn chatted away in a soft Southern drawl: Sam was waiting for us at home; he'd arranged for someone to work for him at the lumberyard; Janey, the elder daughter, had been installed as Worthy Adviser in the Rainbow Girls that weekend—a big event in their lives. Jimmy and Johnny, the boys, would be home for lunch.

The house is set in an oak grove among other ranch houses, not too close together; comfortable and well kept up. Sam's parents live across the street, and their land leads down to the river where Sam built a jetty and sleeping shack for the hot summer nights. "That's the river the song 'Moon River' was about," I was informed.

Sam was coming back from his mother's when we arrived. He is over six feet, broad-shouldered and muscular, and had obviously enjoyed putting back on the thirty pounds he lost in jail. He likes to point out that he is a little over his normal 250 pounds but that it's all muscle, and he certainly gives the impression of being a physically powerful man. Looking at him, then, I could understand why the captain of the plane he had skyjacked took one look at him and said, "We're on our way."

Sam's sandy-red hair is just long enough to curl a little; his complexion is ruddy, even glowing. He looks like a man who spends a lot of time outdoors working with his hands, which he confirmed later with great satisfaction as he pointed out the enclosed Japanese garden he built while awaiting trial.

Sam was smiling when I met him. He smiles with his whole face, crinkling his eyes, and the smile conveys mischief, impulsiveness, and shyness all at once.

One eyelid droops a little, the result of an infection in childhood from a rose-thorn prick. His voice is soft, low, and gentle. Walking around the yard, Sam took the role of the tourist guide: "The head of the John Birch chapter lives over there."

I remembered something a Southern friend of mine had once told me: "Nobody escapes from a Southern childhood without an inbred strain of the 'crazies.'" At first I found it hard to believe that this aging Huckleberry Finn showing me his barbecue imagined himself to be an assassin. I looked closer—was there not a glimmer of that "thousand mile" look in Sam's eyes which would make the bizarre series of events surrounding his skyjacking seem not so implausible?

At lunch we sat beneath some hanging mugs painted

with the insignia of *Apollo 11*. The children came and went, gulping down steak fondue and slices of a giant cake, decorated as an American flag, which had been left over from Janey's Rainbow Girl installation ceremony.

After lunch, Sam got up and went to his room across from the kitchen to pull out all his files on the skyjacking. By the time I walked in, his king-size bed was covered with newspaper clippings, transcriptions of testimony, letters and memorabilia from his stay in Cuba. He showed me the copy of a letter he'd sent to the Levi Straus Company:

> Gentlemen:
>
> On the morning of Jan. 11, 1969, I put on a pair of "Mr. Levi" Sta Press slacks and went to work. At 11 P.M. I arrived in Havana, Cuba, "in a situation beyond my control." I was taken to jail and put in solitary confinement for 109 days. The only clothing I had was what I had on. I lived in these slacks the duration of my confinement. I crawled on my hands and knees until there was no skin on them. After your inspection I would appreciate them being returned to me.
>
> These slacks are as good as new except where my wife cut them in search of a diary I had sewn inside the lining of my pocket.
>
> I highly recommend "Mr. Levi's" to anyone who is confined or travels a lot. As for everyday wear, I think the above is proof enough of the durability. The price is most remarkable for such comfortable and well-styled slacks. Thanks for making them.

Sam assured me that every word he'd written was

true and added that Levi Straus had been so pleased with his endorsement that they had sent him a free pair of slacks.

He shuffled through some more papers, handing me clippings and notes he had taken in Cuba. When he came to a leather folder, the smile on his face vanished. "Seventeen years in the military and they give me this." It was a certificate of discharge from the service, received while he was in Cuba. Since I was not familiar with military discharges, and since this one stated, "General Discharge under honorable circumstances," I wondered why he was so sad. Sam explained that it meant all his time in the military was wiped out—a fate worse than death, so far as he was concerned. "I put everything I had into serving my country," he said grimly, "and I would gladly give up my life for it. I'm not gonna accept this. I got people working on it, congressmen and senators, I'm gonna get reinstated if it's the last thing I do."

It seemed important that I understand what the military meant to him. He had always wanted to be a marine but was underage when he tried to enlist during the Korean War, and his parents wouldn't sign the papers. Enlistments in the Marine Corps were frozen before he came of age, so he joined the Georgia Air National Guard and was sent to Stewart Air Force Base in Nashville. He found the discipline, haphazard training, and general lack of interest in the war a big disappointment. Sam and a friend went AWOL to San Diego, where they tried to smuggle themselves onto a troop ship bound for Korea. No one would help them break through maximum security to the docks ("We didn't know the marine lingo and didn't have the right gear"), and Sam finally gave up when his father broke down and cried during his farewell telephone call. Unable to disobey his father, he turned himself in.

Sam was then deactivated, though he stayed in the reserves while attending the University of Georgia. Upon his discharge in 1954, he promptly joined the Marine Corps Reserve Unit in Savannah. The next ten years seem to have been the best years of Sam's life. The Marine Corps was everything he had dreamed it would be. But his dearest wish was never realized—he was never sent into action. His drill attendance record was perfect, and he attended numerous special training programs that earned him periodic promotions to the rank of staff sergeant. The most important training, he felt, was the Escape, Evasion, and Survival course at Pickle Meadows, California, to which he credits his survival in Cuba. He mentioned with disapproval that a Senate investigation of this particular school, resulting from a complaint of unnecessarily brutal treatment by some politician's son, had forced the army to soften up the course.

"We were Class 1-A combat ready, a real strike force," he said. "They kept us all keyed up with one crisis or another—Lebanon, Berlin. I really believed we would be activated any minute. Then, *wham,* the Defense Department disbands my company. Just like that, the best damn unit in the South, and all of a sudden they just don't need us."

Carolyn walked in and said wearily, "I don't know why they don't send you old men to war and make you happy. None of the young kids seem to want to go, and here he's just dyin' for the chance." She looked at Sam and shook her head: "Go ahead and get yourself killed, but I'll just never understand why."

Sam kept talking in his soft voice, taking me back into Audie Murphy country. In 1964 a recently organized Army Green Beret Unit in Savannah had saved him from despair. Sam, wondering if he'd have the nerve to go through the necessary jump school course, joined a sky-diving club. He found that although the spirit was willing, the body fouled up. He broke his leg. The break required a screw as well as a cast, but it never healed properly because Sam would not curtail his strenuous physical activities and even jumped while still wearing the cast. He went off to airborne training favoring the leg.

He explained to me how parachute landings should be made, but I never did get it straight. I did understand that his weak leg made it impossible for him to make what he called the four-point landing, which absorbs the shock evenly. Sam consistently made a two-point landing—first his feet and then his head.

He was warned that if he used his head as a landing point many more times, he would risk being reduced to a vegetable. He continued to jump, his own way, usually knocking himself unconscious; each time his buddies helped patch him up for the next jump. He was awarded his wings on a stretcher, and he remembers with pride the officer's comment that he'd sure gotten them the hard way.

Sam was alternately exhilarated by his memories and depressed over the waste of his patriotic dedication on the home front. "I felt like such a phony, training all those guys who went off to Korea and Vietnam while I was never even combat-tested." Then he added with some satisfaction, "Until Cuba, that is."

His confinement in Cuba, he insisted, was exactly what he had been trained for in Escape, Evasion, and Survival School—harassment alternating with sympathetic interviews. He seemed proud of his reaction to all their attempts to break him down and chuckled at the memory of how easy it had been to rile up the Cuban guards.

"Once I discovered there was this one spot in my cell where I could crouch down and be hidden from the little view hole in the cell door. See, the guard looks in and he can't find me, so he opens the door real scared now, and there's hardly any light in my cell. He peeks around the door and I come out of my corner with this white sheet draped over my head and going *wooooo, wooooo.* Man, he beat it out of there so fast!"

Carolyn and I laughed at Sam's reenactment of the towering ghost menacing the little Cuban guard. "And tell her about the fingernails," said Carolyn. Sam, obviously enjoying the audience reaction, went into another act.

"Well," he said, "in training they taught us to bite off all our fingernails and tear off our toenails, and then you cup them all together in your hand, all twenty of them, you see, and throw them up in the air." He and Carolyn went into gales of laughter at the expression on my face. "Don't you see?" said Sam. "Then you search for them, and you have to fit each one back on the right nail."

Carolyn added that it took Sam two days to find the

first nail. "He was so tickled he could hardly stand it."

Despite the hilarity, it was clear to me that Sam was just as serious about the fingernail game as he was about all aspects of his military training. When he said, "Throw them up in the air," he meant heave them to kingdom come.

This fascinating conversation about games prisoners play was interrupted by the arrival of Sam's lawyer, who was anxious that I hear about the legal aspects of Sam's trial. We all went into the living room, and Carolyn started telling me her part in the story from the beginning.

She carefully described Sam's head injuries and his increasingly peculiar behavior after being hit by the chain at the lumber mill. The Sunday before the skyjacking, Sam had gone to jump practice, landing once again on his head. He came home with some friends to barbecue some steaks, completely ignoring Carolyn's protests that she had already prepared steak for dinner. At one point in the evening the older son, Jimmy, was cleaning a shotgun in his bedroom. It accidentally went off, blowing holes in the ceiling and scaring Carolyn half to death.

"I called Sam in and he acted as though nothing had happened. Just said, 'Well, clean it up,' and went out again. Then about ten minutes later he came bursting back in and grabbed Jimmy, shaking him and yelling, just having a fit. It took me and two others to separate them. I couldn't understand what had come over him."

I knew from reading his case history that Sam had felt very guilty about this outburst of violence. He brooded all the next week and spent most of his time at work sitting alone in one of the back sheds at the mill. His guilt about what he'd done soon spread to include his failure to test his military training "like my buddies who were in Vietnam," which stirred up resentment about the dependence of employees and family that kept him tied to home. He had told Dr. Hubbard he began to feel unreal, "like I was watching myself do things, but couldn't do anything about it."

Carolyn continued to put more pieces of the puzzle together for me. The evening of the skyjacking, Sam came home distracted and withdrawn. Carolyn, who had been working in her father's store all afternoon, was tired and preoccupied. Sam made the cryptic announcement that he could make a quarter of a million dollars if he just had the courage, and went into his bedroom, leaving her curious but too tired to pursue the mystery.

Sam came out of the bedroom with the briefcase he always took to reserve meetings and said he was going to Jacksonville. "Now I knew he didn't have any business in Jacksonville, so I decided to outbluff him and said, 'Okay, then, I'm going with you.'" She bundled up Jenny and got in the car. Sam asked her to drive to the home of Lieutenant Lee, a member of Sam's reserve unit, but no one was home when they got there.

"If he'd been home, I probably wouldn't have gone," Sam interjected, "and then again," he added, "he might have gone with me." Sam had a way of saying something unexpected in a way that always provoked laughter, but I was beginning to suspect that he might be serious and at the same time might find laughter an appropriate response to whatever he was saying.

The three of them then drove to the family store, where Sam took a gun out of the case by the cash register. Carolyn asked him why he wanted the gun, which they both knew was broken beyond repair. Sam made a joke about wanting to go frog hunting with it. Listening to Carolyn describe this exchange, I had the impression that by this time in their marriage, she was so used to Sam's erratic behavior that she never pressed very hard for explanations.

At this point I interrupted to ask Sam why he hadn't taken one of his own guns. He explained that although he had owned six or seven handguns, he had given them all away about a month before the skyjacking. He still didn't understand why he'd done it, but he had replaced them and now had what struck me as a staggering list of firearms in his present collection. Carolyn added, "You should have seen the face of that FBI agent when he came to search the house after Sam skyjacked. There were rifles and shotguns all over the place."

Sam laughed. "I even got the same kind of rifle Lee Harvey Oswald used to kill Kennedy. That really freaked them out."

They all got back in the car with the broken gun and started driving into town, at which point Sam very calmly began to tell Carolyn about his "mission."

"He said he had been appointed by the CIA and FBI to take part in a conspiracy to overthrow the Castro regime," she recounted, "and that he had to be in Cuba before the Johnson administration went out of office. He said things like, 'You know about all those people who are shot trying to escape from Cuba,' and

'We cannot let this continue.' He told me he'd be gone from four to six months, and that while he was away I would hear nothing from him, it would be like he'd just vanished. I said, 'Well, Sam, these people will kill you.' And he said, 'Don't worry, everything's been arranged. I'll be out of there on a boat and I don't know where I'll turn up—it could be Canada, Russia, Red China. . . .' "

Carolyn confessed that none of this made any sense to her at the time, but when she protested, Sam said, "You *know* how I feel about my country." Carolyn agreed. "And yes, I knew how he felt and I also knew that *had* he been assigned to do something like that, he would have done it." But she maintained she was only half convinced that Sam was serious when she left him off at his captain's house. "And he never once mentioned to me that he was going to hijack, just that he was part of a conspiracy and that he would be *on* a hijacked airplane."

In an attempt to separate the threads of reality out of this web of fantasy, I asked Carolyn at what point she had realized that Sam wasn't part of a CIA plot and had imagined the whole thing. "I'm still not convinced," she said softly.

I thought I wasn't hearing right, but she went on to explain that there were still too many questions that hadn't been answered to her satisfaction. Sam grinned and said, "I still haven't collected the quarter of a million yet"; Carolyn gazed at him with that "thousand mile" look and an "I know what I know" expression.

With this impasse I decided I'd better approach reality from another direction. Sam must know that it was just plain crazy to think he could have pulled off an assassination with a broken gun and no assurance whatsoever that he would ever come face to face with Castro in the first place.

"You realize now that those were absurd expectations, don't you?" I stated more than asked, confident that he would agree with me and set Carolyn straight. Sam looked disappointed—apparently at my poverty of insight.

"No, I could have done it," he assured me. "I didn't need a gun, that was just to get the plane to Cuba because I had no intention of harming anyone on that plane."

He then very gently explained to his slow-witted pupil that Castro always travels with a phalanx of eight guards. "I was going to disarm one of the guards and shoot Castro. I would have been killed, too, but I could have got to him before they got me." Simple as that.

I began to wonder if it was *my* grip on reality that was slipping. I glanced at the lawyer, who appeared to be having a quiet fit in the corner, and was a little reassured. I tried again. "But, Sam, whatever made you think that Castro would come and meet your airplane? He just doesn't *do* that."

"Yes, he does," Sam said patiently. "He came to meet that 747 that was skyjacked. I know I could have done it if everything had gone right."

The lawyer interrupted to say he had another appointment, which gave me a few moments to regain my composure. I decided to abandon any rational approach: it was clear that I wasn't making any more sense to

Sam and Carolyn than they were to me. They had not been offended by my obvious surprise and increasing disbelief in the events they were describing; they both seemed to feel that I would understand if only they could find the right words.

While I was mulling over these thoughts, Sam talked quietly about patriotism. Words often failed Sam on this subject; he would let a sentence trail off, then shake his head and smile in an effort to keep his feelings under control. He was aware that many people would find his unquestioning dedication square, but he kept reminding me that he was a Depression baby. His father's stories about suffering through those lean years and then achieving the American dream through frugality and hard work had impressed in Sam a deep sense of gratitude. "I was always brought up believing in God and country, apple pie and Momma, you know," he laughed, "and how thankful we should be." There just never seemed to be any way to pay his dues to his satisfaction, which brought Sam back to his old obsession about being a phony—not combat-tested.

Sam concluded this simplistic but oddly touching testimony of faith on an unexpected note: "But I found out in Cuba that we aren't the guys in the white hats after all." Mistaking my surprise for disapproval, he hastily explained. "I mean, we fall a lot short. But it's still the greatest country in the world, no question about it."

Carolyn called us to dinner, and the realization that I was very hungry restored my equilibrium. Sam was subdued during the meal, and when we went into the living room afterward, he seemed depressed. It was like talking to a different person—no jokes, no bravado—which I found more disturbing than his super-patriotism.

"I don't go to church anymore because they don't have any answers. I used to believe in all that, but I know now it isn't true. Dr. Hubbard was right about feeling guilty, and my parents, and wanting to get killed—all that. I guess I felt so bad I just wanted to die."

Sam hunched down in his chair, momentarily bereft of his dreams, projecting an overwhelming sense of loss. I asked him how surviving his confinement in Cuba had affected him. "Didn't that prove to you that maybe you wanted to live after all?" I asked hopefully.

My question only seemed to remind him of the meaning he had found in the Cubans' lives. In jail he had been given books to read by Castro and Ché Guevara, along with Communist textbooks. "We weren't the guys in the white hats when we exploited *that* country. I can see what they're doing now. Some of them were beautiful, really beautiful. They had a dedication to a cause that puts us to shame. People helping each other—they had respect. It was really beautiful."

When I asked him if he still wanted to kill Castro, he said, "No, I understand what he's up against now."

Sam rambled on about how the United States had lost its way somehow, no longer inspiring the kind of dedication he had found and envied in Cuba.

Then suddenly he switched from the Cubans to the Palestinian skyjackings. "Why didn't one of those crew members offer himself as a hostage, even if it meant he would be killed, so the Arabs would let the others go? I can't understand the cowardice, the lack of purpose, in those guys. Not one of them was willing to put his life on the line. Every one of those Cubans would die for his way of life."

I suggested that Sam had perhaps misinterpreted the Palestinians' motive, which had been to deal an economic and psychological blow to the West: "They even gave up their own lives to protect the hostages during the Jordanian army attacks." This news depressed Sam even more—the Palestinians were willing to die for their cause, too.

Everything I said seemed to make matters worse. All the fight had gone out of Sam. As he hunched deeper and deeper in his chair, he seemed to be diminishing physically as well as spiritually. I began to miss the fantasies.

As Carolyn came in the room, Sam made a sign that he didn't want her to hear him talking that way and snapped out of his mood. When I mentioned that I was still wondering why Sam's reserve captain had driven him to the airport, Sam jumped up and said, "Let's go and ask him." We all climbed into the car to collect the captain, who had been located at the country club shooting craps.

Sam went into the club while Carolyn and I waited in the car. Carolyn, who had noticed Sam's depression despite his efforts to cover it up, said she was worried about his moods. She felt that he was reading too much, by which she meant that books gave him funny ideas. "And there's another thing that bothers me," she said. "He's never once said he was sorry for what he did. He doesn't seem to feel it was wrong."

"Is that one of the reasons you think the story of the plot might be true?" I asked her.

"That and other things. You see, his father received a phone call just after Sam went, from some man who said he was a judge or something in Florida. And he said something about not trying to get in touch with Sam, that he was okay and not to do anything. And he did come back when he said he would, the way he said he would. And he did get acquitted even though he was guilty. Oh, I don't know, there are so many questions in my mind I can't find any answers for," Carolyn sighed.

Thinking of Sam's trial, I wondered to myself if Carolyn seriously thought the jurors could have been in on the plot, too. I knew I was slipping again when a voice in my head said the government moves in mysterious ways.

"And then last fall," Carolyn went on, "he wanted to go over to those Arabs or whoever they are. Now that just didn't make any sense at all." It didn't to me, either, and Carolyn explained patiently. "Oh, you know, when he tried to get a message to those Arabs who skyjacked all those airplanes and kept the passengers. He wanted to offer himself as a hostage if they would let the passengers go. Of course, we stopped him and told him he couldn't do that, but it got me real upset."

A conversation I'd had with a sky marshal right after the Palestinian skyjackings suddenly replayed itself in my mind. I'd asked him what had made him become a sky marshal. "The President asked for help," he explained with pride.

"Do you really think you could prevent another Palestinian-type skyjacking?"

"No. And I'm really afraid, because they have threatened to skyjack a plane with us on it and castrate us." This delivered in hushed tones.

"I've never heard *that.* What would you do?"

"I would go up to them and present my gun and credentials and tell them to do what they want to me just as long as they free the passengers and crew," he said bravely. Whereupon he informed me seriously, without a hint of irony in his voice, that he had eight children.

I was startled out of my reverie by the sight of Sam and Billy, his reserve captain, running out of the club and jumping into the car. It was raining now, but Billy was in high spirits, and the atmosphere of the car was immediately charged with his exuberance. Outside our windows a strong wind snatched at the beards on the oak trees, and a bolt of lightning ripped across the sky. I looked at Billy, who hadn't stopped talking since he got in the car.

Even under normal circumstances it would have taken no small effort to follow Billy's headlong sentences and Southern accent. His round face was super-animated as he asked me a string of questions without bothering to wait for the answers. Since I was anything but sure of just what was going on at that moment, I was happy to have Billy fill up all the silences. I did manage to establish the fact that I was writing a book on skyjacking, which reminded Billy of a magazine article that described his part in putting Sam on the plane and, as Billy put it, quoted him out of context. "*Boy* did *I* sound *stupid.* This dumb captain puts *Sam* on the plane so's he can hijack to Cuba. Whew!" Billy laughed with us, then expressed some anxiety about what I intended to do to his image.

By the time we got back to the house, Billy had apparently decided that I had an honest face. When he announced that he'd be happy to give me any information he could, Sam laughed and said, "I still can't figure out why you let me go down there. So tell it like it was, I'm not gonna get all choked up if you say I was a bullshitter."

Billy looked stricken, said, "Oh, mah God, then it was all my fault," and launched into his story while Sam brought him the first of several beers. Billy first told me that he had been too preoccupied with preparations for a hunting trip the next day to pay much attention to Sam rambling on about being part of a revolutionary force that was to overthrow Castro. "After all," he explained, "not only has Sam always done unusual things, but more often than that he has talked about unusual things that he was going to do, or had done, that never really *did* take place."

Billy admitted that Sam had been acting more strangely than usual, but he'd put it down to a combination of Sam's normal craziness and his overenthusiastic patriotism. He expected Sam to "knock off the act" any moment and start laughing the way he often did when he was indulging in his favorite sport of putting people on. And so Billy continued to play along with Sam as he drove him to the airport, half listening to Sam's instructions that the FBI be contacted after four days. Billy swore that Sam never mentioned sky-jacking a plane until they were at the airport. He added —rather incongruously for someone who hadn't taken the fantasy seriously—that he'd assumed Sam was going to Cuba on one of those refugee flights that left from Miami every day. By now I was getting used to this sort of doublethink.

"Hell," said Billy, "I came just short of going with him, 'cause the Super Bowl was the next day in Miami, and Sam offered to buy me a plane ticket. I really thought he was pulling my leg and was going down to the Super Bowl. So if I hadn't been going on this real great hunting trip the next day, I would probably have gone with him. Hell, I don't know if I'd have been an accomplice or just a spectator." His eyes bugged out at the thought of his close call with this highly illegal drama.

Billy admitted to some misgivings at the ticket counter, where Sam made a big scene about his non-existent reservation and bought a one-way ticket with cash. "That was the only shred of doubt in my mind. I thought, *well,* if someone *was* going to hijack a plane, all of a sudden it occurred to me that this might be the way they would act. So on this hand Sam was perfectly capable of hijacking a plane, and on that hand he was one hundred percent *more* capable of joking about it but not doing it." At this point Billy had put his doubts out of his mind and told Sam to enjoy the Super Bowl. He was a little annoyed when Sam kept up his act to the end, even giving Billy his Masonic ring with instructions to hand it over to Carolyn for the children.

When he got home, "just to make sure," Billy called Carolyn, who told him that Sam was on a mission for the CIA and warned him not to say anything about it. Billy couldn't bring himself to believe that Sam had forced a plane to Cuba, even after he read about the skyjacking in the newspaper. He decided to repeat Sam's story to the FBI—half hoping that they would confirm it, giving Sam's behavior some meaning. Sensing how much he wanted to believe that his friend was on a mission and not crazy, the FBI sent an agent out to see Billy.

"This guy says, 'I want to tell you this off the record. Now the FBI and CIA have both done some way-out things, but among the way-out things we would not do is to send Sam, who has a history of doing unusual and crazy things, down there to assassinate Castro. That is something we would definitely not do. Think of it like this. Suppose the FBI had hired him to do that, they would still tell you that they didn't. Nobody would ever tell you that Yes we hired him to do this, so we're gonna tell you that we didn't do this whether we did or we didn't. But let me assure you that we *didn't.*' "

Billy then claimed that he was personally very much opposed to people skyjacking airplanes—"except for Sam, 'cause I figure he's a good guy, you know, and he shouldn't be punished. I was glad he got off because he was temporarily insane." Billy grinned and added, " 'Course, some people think that's the greatest compliment anybody ever paid Sam, to say he was only *temporarily* insane." This comment provoked a "Thanks a lot" from Sam and laughter from the rest of us.

Sam drove Billy back to his crap game while Carolyn and I talked awhile before going to bed. She told me about the time Sam had climbed into a tall tree and hooted like an owl, adding a little sadly, "but he doesn't do things like that anymore."

I was to sleep in Sam's room, whose walls are decorated with photographs of himself on reserve maneuvers and an oil painting of him in his Green Beret uniform. I walked over to read a piece of paper stuck in the oil painting. It was a quote from Theodore Roosevelt:

> Far better it is to dare mighty things, to win glorious triumphs, even though checkered with failure, than to take rank with those poor spirits who neither enjoy much nor suffer much, because they live in the grey twilight that knows not victory nor defeat.

The next morning Sam and I sat around the breakfast table talking about his trip back from Cuba. He was greatly disturbed that the majority of the passengers were Americans who had been to revolutionary training schools down there and were returning through Canada with the intention of organizing a revolution in the United States. He conveyed just a hint of admiration for the revolutionaries' dedication and a great deal of frustration that nothing was being done to stop them.

When I asked him if he would still assassinate Castro given the chance, Sam nodded enthusiastically and said "Sure."

It occurred to me that patriotism acted like a narcotic on Sam. If our gloomy session of the previous evening had been any clue to what kicking the habit would do to him, I preferred the addiction but wished there were some way to make sure he only got maintenance doses. There is certainly no doubt in Sam's mind about what he would die for. It is his insistence that he be allowed to prove it that is so alarming.

When it was time for me to leave, I looked at my ticket and mentioned that I had to change planes in Atlanta. Sam grinned and said softly, "Well, honey, if you want a direct flight, I've got a gun you can borrow."

I laughed at this outrageous bit of humor, then recovered and said, "Sam, you are incorrigible."

Sam blushed and looked at his feet. "Yeah," he said. "I reckon I am."

The last time I saw Sam he was in New York. While we were having a drink in his hotel bar, he told me about the hate mail and telephone calls he had been receiving as a result of a television interview. Predictably, he had tried on the show to explain to Mr. and Mrs. America that he really could have killed Castro. Carolyn and the children were bewildered and frightened at the public response, and Sam was upset by all the people who were calling him crazy. I tried to explain gently that his stubborn insistence on convincing the world would be bound to strike other people as crazy, but after listening politely to my explanations Sam left to make another appearance on television. Seeing him go, I sensed once again the triumph of hope over experience: if only he could find the right words, *somebody* would understand.

7

THE VIETNAM WAR is now woven into our lives like a piece of barbed wire. Not surprisingly, it cuts and jags its way through the subject of skyjacking as the public manifestation—and scapegoat—of private nightmares and fears. With Sam the war and his distance from its real battles serve as a front for his failure to face himself.

For George the war is more symbol than scapegoat. Convinced that his privileged life has corrupted him, he suffers from a familiar liberal malaise which paralyzes him, making participation in a capitalistic society difficult and an active role in changing it impossble. Unable to come to terms privately with this society, George finds in the war his hopes—and fears—that poverty and purpose will provide the inner strength to triumph eventually over the force of corrupted money and power. The way George sees it, he stands to get crushed by both sides just trying to be a nice guy.

Raffaele Miniciello is still another story. A decorated marine veteran of the Vietnam War, he started out a dedicated GI fighting for the free, capitalist way of life and ended up by skyjacking to his fatherland, a surprised but not entirely unwilling socialist hero.

That, at least, is the public face of it all. Raffaele has been fed the story so many times by Italian guardians with tenuous socialist connections and deep-rooted capitalist ambitions that he can dish out the elementary political rhetoric without any prompting. Apparently everyone in Italy feels free to exalt and exploit Raffaele for one universal purpose—to make money. How did a sweet, naïve Italian immigrant get himself in such a predicament?

Raffaele grew up in the dusty, sun-bleached village of Melito Irpino, not far from Naples by miles but years distant in progress and activity. Nothing much ever happens or changes in Melito Irpino. Raffaele's skyjacking was the most exciting event since the eruption of Mount Vesuvius.

His father was one of the village's more sophisticated residents by virtue of United States citizenship obtained during a period spent working in the United States many years earlier. Raffaele remembers his father as stern, authoritarian, and distant; his mother as docile and devout.

When Raffaele was thirteen, the family moved back to the United States, where his eager but inadept attempts to learn a new language were met with the indifference of busy adults and the petty cruelties of cliquey teen-agers. "My mother speak to me in Italian and my father don't take the time to help me. Nobody care except one teacher in the library but she don't have enough time." To make matters worse, Raffaele's sister was quick to learn English and found Raffaele's clumsy attempts more cause for embarrassment than for sympathetic help.

School became an agony of alienation and torment. Raffaele never dated girls because he was too shy to ask them out. His efforts in school were rewarded with rebuffs and impatience, and he began playing hooky. Healthy and muscular, he at least was good at sports, particularly wrestling, but even this pleasure was marred by emotional conflict. "I went out for wrestling at Foster High, and I was good. But I didn't know if I wanted to win or lose. If I won, I felt sorry for the other guy. And if I lose, I think that's not good. I didn't try. I should of won. And I would get mad." At sixteen Raffaele gave up trying in studies and sports and quit school.

He went to work full-time in a supermarket, waiting for the day he would be seventeen and eligible to join the marines. "I really thought that we were doing right over there. I believe what they tell me about the gooks and Commies, I felt proud to fight for my country." Raffaele's unquestioning convictions were based on a combination of elementary schoolboy history and marine indoctrination.

He was happy to get away from home, because his sister's success in school and increasing hostility to him had been a constant humiliation. "You know what she tell me the day I go to Vietnam? She said, 'I hope you get killed.' I don't know why she hate me." The horrors of Vietnam slowly ate away Raffaele's pride in his uniform. He fought the seasoned cynicism of older troops for a time but finally opted for the familiar escape of grass and pills. He began to feel that maybe he had more kinship with the "gooks" than with some of his buddies, whose every irritation was expressed in terms like "dirty wop." His faith in the Church faltered when it became clear just how cheap life was, especially his. "The leaders of my platoon just think of me as cannon fodder. I really get mad. Always, they send me first up the road with the mine sweeper so they can walk safe and not get blown up. 'Send the wop,' they say."

Aside from joining his buddies in popping a few pills and smoking grass, Raffaele was a model soldier. He obeyed commands with quiet resentment and earned routine promotions and decorations for staying alive and doing his duty.

Since there was nothing he wanted to spend his pay on in Vietnam, he had the Marine Corps withhold one hundred dollars a month in a government savings account—until he heard that misappropriation of these funds was not uncommon. Deposit slips rarely reach the battlefront; and without such tangible proof, his buddies told him, he was sure not to get back as much as he had put in. Acting on their advice, Raffaele had the deduction stopped after eight months.

After a year in Vietnam he was assigned to Camp Pendleton in California. He decided to take his money out of the government account and put it in a more reliable place. True to his buddies' predictions, the paymaster insisted that he had only six hundred of the eight hundred dollars coming to him. When he refused even to look up the records, Raffaele was outraged. His immediate reaction was to decide that if they could steal his money, he had the right to steal it back. The idea incubated over a period of months. A half-dozen beers gave him the courage to carry out a logical but highly illegal plan of action: he broke into the base PX and carefully selected two hundred dollars' worth of merchandise. Unfortunately, the beers had also made navigation difficult: Raffaele lay down in the adjoining recreation hall, surrounded by his booty, and took a little nap. He was awakened by two MP's. Instead of being thrown into the stockade, he was booked in a San Diego civil court and released pending trial. Overcrowded court dockets made it impossible to schedule his case for several months, by which time Raffaele had all but forgotten about the incident. In the meantime he had been to paratrooper training and was very proud to have earned his wings. Inclusion in this elite corps restored some of the military glamour that his tour in Vietnam had tarnished. Raffaele was willing to forgive and forget.

And it seemed as though that was the way it was going to be. The day of the trial, a marine lawyer took him to the San Diego court and explained the circumstances to the judge. The judge, taking into consideration the fact that Raffaele's attempt at personal justice had only cost the military one broken lock, decided to drop the case. Raffaele felt somewhat vindicated and cheerfully went with his lawyer to the colonel's office to report the outcome.

The colonel, less compassionate than the judge, immediately ordered his secretary to type up a court-martial. All the rage and resentment Raffaele had felt over the original injustice boiled up again as he slowly realized that this man was determined to convict him.

The colonel instructed the lawyer to tell Raffaele to plead guilty or face a six-month sentence and a bad-conduct discharge. The trial was set for October 31.

During September and October, Raffaele brooded about his dilemma. He was innocent; he knew he *couldn't* plead guilty. He also knew that if he didn't, the colonel would give him the full sentence, and he'd have to carry a bad record for the rest of his life. There was no justice under these rules.

He knew that in Italy things wouldn't be settled this way. There a man would die before relinquishing his honor. As the date for the court-martial drew closer, Raffaele found himself in a state of confusion and murderous rage. The problem no longer seemed to be whether or not to plead guilty, but how to escape to his hometown in Italy—where people shared his sense of justice—or die trying. Raffaele hadn't lived in Melito Irpino for thirteen years for nothing. He knew these Italians' Old World values would mean understanding and acceptance.

He insists that if he could have gotten a passport, he would have flown to Italy without resorting to the unorthodox method of skyjacking and is insulted that people think he stole an airplane because he couldn't afford a ticket. In fact, the night before the trial he withdrew all his money, some $460, and paid a buddy $50 to replace him on guard duty. He then bought an M-1 carbine, 250 rounds of ammunition, and the provisions he'd need while hiding out in the Italian countryside. With this equipment he set out for Los Angeles, vaguely determined to skyjack an airplane. There didn't seem to be any other way.

He boarded TWA's Flight 85 to San Francisco at Los Angeles International Airport. After bolstering his courage with two whiskeys, he assembled his gun and informed the hostess that he wanted to go to New York. Let into the cockpit, he delivered his message to the captain, whose response was, "You've just chartered yourself an airplane." Raffaele was impressed. Until that moment, Italy had been a far-off dream, less real than the conviction that he would be killed.

It was one of the longest skyjackings in history. The plane first landed in Denver, where Raffaele allowed the passengers and crew to deplane. One hostess, perhaps feeling that her presence had a calming effect on this skyjacker—but also, she later stated with spectacular cool, because she wanted to go to New York—volunteered to remain on board. An hour later the plane flew to New York to pick up an international crew, then took off before refueling because Raffaele had panicked at the obvious attempts of the FBI to flush him out in the open so they could get a shot at him. He says his gun went off accidentally in the cockpit, frightening him as much as the crew, who took off precipitously, believing their lives to be in danger. They landed in Bangor, Maine, to refuel, which was accomplished without incident, and headed for Shannon, Ireland, still unaware of the final destination.

During the long ride across the Atlantic, Raffaele was kept company by Tracy Coleman, the hostess, and Captain Cook, the pilot who had flown Flight 85 to New York and remained on board. Raffaele had been mysterious about where he wanted to go—first, it was New York, then, inexplicably, Cairo—perhaps because he figured the less time the Italian police had to prepare for him, the better; or perhaps because he was so sure he was going to die that he didn't really think he'd reach any desired destination. Raffaele is still confused about this.

The turning point in his expectations came when he put his gun down on the seat and walked unarmed all the way to the back of the plane. He was bewildered and perhaps a little disappointed when Captain Cook didn't pick it up and shoot him. His chances for survival looked even better when the captain told him that although he didn't want to die, he didn't want to kill Raffaele either. Raffaele, suddenly conscious-stricken over making the crew fear for their lives, assured Captain Cook and Tracy that he would take his own life before harming them. To dramatize the way he would do it, he stuck the gun under his chin. Captain Cook hastily assured him that he would prefer the flight to terminate without *anyone* getting hurt.

Once Raffaele figured out his escape from the Rome airport, his demands were radioed ahead. The Italian officials complied and had a car with an unarmed driver waiting to transport him into the countryside. Already, vague information about his background and war record were being broadcast worldwide. Uncertain as to how dangerous he was, the Italian news media reacted with a mixture of sympathy and apprehension—Raffaele was characterized as a native son, brutalized by the Vietnam War, gone berserk.

Before leaving the plane, Raffaele apologized to the crew for putting them to so much trouble. To everybody's relief he was then driven off by an assistant chief of the airport police who had volunteered to go along unarmed. The carabinieri picked him up in a field the next day, November 1, as he was wandering around in a state of confusion. It was his twentieth birthday.

Raffaele served a year and a half of a seven-year sentence, after a trial that was characterized by melodramatic defense and reluctant prosecution. The Italian government had refused to extradite Raffaele to the United States—officially on the grounds of a law forbidding extradition to countries that impose the death penalty for the crime committed; unofficially on the grounds that Raffaele had become a popular hero and national treasure. His story was written, broadcast on radio, and televised as that of a modern-day Don Quixote victimized by an imperialist American war machine. Movie rights were sold. Marriage proposals poured in, and the Roman tabloids ran stories in which movie starlets and models tearfully confessed their love for him.

While the press and publicity mongers were enjoying the fruits of Raffaele's spectacular story, Raffaele sat in Refine Coili prison, serving out his sentence. His mother moved back to Melito Irpino to wait for her son's release; his father, whom he had vaguely hoped to join when he began the skyjacking, died while Raffaele was in jail.

In April, 1971, I asked a friend who was gathering material for a television program on skyjacking if he knew how one went about getting permission to see Raffaele. His Rome office contacted the Italian authorities and sent back the surprising news that no permission from the government was required—Raffaele was being released from prison in two weeks.

Flying Scared

My elation at Raffaele's accessibility lost altitude when I started reading newspaper items planted by Raffaele's lawyer, mentioning the lawsuits slapped on anyone using Raffaele's story without permission, i.e., suitable payment. But I had nothing to lose by trying, so I flew to Rome and took a taxi to the lawyer's apartment. Informed that Raffaele was not there, I left a copy of my previous book as credentials and a note proposing an interview and asking him to call me at my hotel or, I added frivolously, in New York.

I waited with not much hope for the phone to ring until late that afternoon and then took a flight back to New York.

At four o'clock the next morning, dead asleep in my apartment thanks to jet lag and exhaustion, I heard my telephone ring again and again. When I finally answered, a voice with a lilting Italian accent asked me if I would accept a collect call from Raffaele in Rome. Before I could gather my wits enough to say, "Certainly," an eager wide-awake voice cried from my receiver, "Elizabeta, where are you?" Too sleepy to be sure of the answer, I didn't respond. "Why did you go away? Come back, I want to see you."

I mumbled a reply, grabbed a pen, scribbled a telephone number on my pillowcase, and, presumably, hung up the phone—I don't remember doing it. I woke up late the next day with the vaguest memory of a dream telephone call, but the blurry number written on the pillowcase testified to its reality.

Following a call to Raffaele and some futile attempts to fly to Rome when he was there, I finally arranged to work a flight that coincided with his schedule. In the course of another transatlantic phone call he assured me that German, Italian, and American television had finally finished their programs on him. He would be waiting for me. In fact, he said, his lawyer and he would meet my flight. Visions of paparazzi and television cameras recording the skyjacker hero warmly welcoming a hostess of the very airline he'd borrowed a plane from danced in my head. No, no, I insisted, that wouldn't be necessary.

I was changing out of my uniform in my hotel room in Rome when the telephone rang. "I am downstairs," announced Raffaele. He was waiting for me in the bar-café, easily recognizable from his photographs—he has the husky physique and coarse, handsome features of a high-school football hero. I introduced myself, and Raffaele beamed an eager, nervous smile at me. He stepped outside the hotel entrance and brought back his lawyer, who doesn't speak English. Since I don't speak Italian, I shook his hand and waited for Raffaele to tell me what his lawyer was telling him so excitedly. I assumed he would bring up the subject of money, never before having given away an interview with Raffaele.

Raffaele began to translate earnestly. "My lawyer wants to know if you could get him a date with a hostess. Then we could all go out to dinner tonight." Ah, the glamour of dating an airline hostess had overcome greed. For once in my career I appreciated the effect this myth has on men. The lawyer looked at me expectantly, blinding me with a smile that showed all of his incredibly white teeth. With his silver-flecked wavy hair, expertly tailored suit, and slender build, he was a caricature of Roman elegance. To complete the picture, he clicked his heels and kissed my hand.

Before I could start worrying about how to fulfill his request, a pretty French hostess I had worked the flight with came sauntering across the street, eating cherries out of a bag. Anick fluttered her eyelashes and gave the lawyer a charming smile as she offered him some cherries. His eyes went limpid with admiration. A polyglot conversation ensued, during which it was arranged that she would join us for dinner after Raffaele and I had had some time to talk.

At five that afternoon Raffaele was again waiting for me in the hotel bar. I was sipping a capuccino when he startled me by asking, "Is it true that the TWA pilots want to kidnap me and take me back to the United States to face the death penalty?" I told him I had never heard such a suggestion, but if he was seriously worried about the possibility, we had picked the wrong place to meet. As I talked I recognized three pilots walking out the door, and five others were having drinks across the room from us. Raffaele seemed alarmed when I pointed them out, but he had to agree with me that none of them looked the least bit interested in him. On the other hand, I didn't want to test the degree of hostility any of these pilots might feel toward Raffaele, so I suggested that we go someplace else for the interview. Raffaele told the taxi driver to take us to the Piazza del Poppolo.

There is a café in this piazza where all the trendy Romans go to be seen, and I assumed this would be our destination. Raffaele surprised me by heading for the monument in the middle of the piazza, where we sat on blazing hot concrete while he described the series of events leading up to the skyjacking. He proudly showed me his paratrooper's wings, which he still wears on his watchband, then walked me across the river while he voiced his confusion about his hero image. "I don't like to go to those places where everybody knows me," he said. "It's not true that I am a hero. I only did it because I had no choice. I am just an ordinary boy."

Raffaele, like Sam, Gladys, and George, is unrepentant about his crime, convinced that circumstances forced him to commit it. Now he would like to put all that behind him and get on with his life—sort of. When I asked what he intended to do next, Raffaele informed me that he was going to be a photojournalist. "I have a friend who is a photographer, and we are going to North Vietnam where I will go to the battlefront and send back pictures to show the world what is happening. Maybe I get killed, but the world should know what is going on." It sounded like one of Sam's harebrained schemes to be a dead hero. I argued that the world had already been exposed to countless photographs of the Vietnam slaughter, which apparently left the decision-makers unmoved.

Raffaele listened but remained adamant in his conviction that his pictures would open everybody's eyes. "Maybe I get killed," he said again happily, "but I must live by my ideals." It was obvious that like thousands of other veterans, Raffaele had been deeply disturbed by the senseless waste of human life during his tour. But it was equally obvious that his undigested political rhetoric had been fed to him by his lawyer, whose elegant way of life and profit-obsessed approach to business make him one of the most unlikely socialists I've ever met. Certainly Raffaele's image as the socialist hero who humbled the United States is contradictory to his own belief in his skyjacking as a personal response to a very specific affront to his honor. He is too unsophisticated and insecure to find any reassurance in being celebrated symbolically. What's more, as a man who feels he took his own fate in his hands, he is not at all happy to be portrayed as a helpless victim.

He talked of his affection for his lawyer, whom he idolizes and appears to forgive everything. From my brief meeting with the lawyer that morning, it seemed hard to imagine two more unlikely constant companions. While Raffaele did have periodic flashes of anger about being exploited, he directed none of it at the man who had managed with the virtuosity of a Hollywood PR man to turn Raffaele into a highly prized commodity—television programs, a book, magazine articles, and even a contract for the leading role in an Italian western. Listening to the list of deals, I was thankful the lawyer wasn't American—there'd be Raffaele T-shirts, Raffaele dolls, and a chain of pizza stands called Raffjacks.

Raffaele was most happy and relaxed when he was talking about his new apartment, which he will share with his mother. He is very proud that he is able to assume responsibility for her. His sister's continued unfriendliness still troubles him, but he dismisses it, saying she is interested only in herself. He added the stunning bit of news that she was at that moment training with an international airline to be a stewardess. Not thinking, I told him he'd be eligible for free passes as a member of her family. "But where could I go?" he said sadly.

Raffaele continued to participate in things of an aviational, although legitimate, nature. He told me he was going sky-diving the next week and that a friend often gave him rides in his private plane. And he added that if he hadn't disqualified himself so unequivocally, his ideal career would have been that of an airline pilot.

We made our way back to the hotel to pick up Anick and then went on to the lawyer's apartment, where the lawyer and some friends were watching the national election results. The socialists were losing a significant number of seats to the neofascists; but the lawyer's spirits were revived immediately at the sight of Anick, and he put aside politics in favor of romance.

Another polyglot conversation ensued to decide on the restaurant. Raffaele begged for a plain trattoria, supported by Anick and me. The lawyer and a high-spirited male secretary vetoed this suggestion, and we all wedged ourselves into the Alfa-Romeo (because the Ferrari was sick, or the other way around), screeching off at a terrific speed to the al fresco section of a well-known tourist spot. There were wandering opera singers and a menu four feet long, offering that Italian specialty **New York Steak: $8.00** in bold-face type.

I shouldn't complain because the setting gave me a chance to observe Raffaele's public image. As we crossed the threshold, three waiters dropped everything and ran to wring his hand. He smiled uncomfortably and thanked them for their congratulations. The maître d' escorted us to a table, reluctantly seating us in a fairly secluded spot at Raffaele's request. He sat beside a tall hedge, nestling himself inconspicuously among the foliage, but waiters continued to come over and pump his hand.

Across the table from us, the lawyer and his amanuensis flanked Anick, smothering her with the effusive charm that Italian men display toward all women except their wives. Periodically, Raffaele would try to emulate their braggadocio, but since his performance pleased himself least of all, he would soon retreat into the leaves and look at me with unhappy eyes. I asked why he seemed so upset, and he said again that he didn't like "these fancy places"; that he didn't know what people wanted from him. Something else was bothering him. Having signed the contract to star in a western, he was already disenchanted with the film industry. "I don't like these people, and I have asked my lawyer to get me out of the contract. I can't work with people like that, they are all kinds like homosexuals and bad people." He shuddered at the thought of them. "And this girl, I go out with her," he continued. "I think she like me and then she tell me that she is lesbian and only wants to go out with me because I am famous and it would be good for her career if she be seen with me. She offer to pay me to take her out." Raffaele looked heartbroken over his disillusionment, and I remembered that he had been too shy to ask girls out as a teen-ager.

The lawyer chose this moment to ask me what I thought of skyjacking. With Raffaele's help I managed to explain that I thought governments ought to throw away the principle of political asylum and deny sanctuary to all skyjackers so we wouldn't be faced with deciding who was a "good" skyjacker and who was a "bad" one. As gently as I could, I explained that the act of skyjacking should be judged medically rather than politically or morally.

Considering Raffaele's freshly induced depression from the sad tale of the lesbian girl friend, I felt guilty about putting him in the position of translating these opinions. Keeping the conversation as theoretical as possible, I asked Raffaele if he would have skyjacked had he known he would be returned to the United States immediately. After insisting a number of times that he had been forced to do it, he admitted that he would not have skyjacked under those circumstances. Even as he conceded my point, I could see that he was morbidly contemplating his alternative: death. In an attempt to cheer him up, I reminded him of something he had told me that afternoon.

With some satisfaction he'd announced that the colonel who had court-martialed him was in prison on a hit-and-run driving charge. "I know now that I could have gone to someone higher than the colonel and reported him and that I wouldn't have had to plead guilty, but I didn't know that then. I didn't think I had a chance." I pointed out that if he had faced his court-martial, he might not have been found guilty, despite the colonel, and that a guilty verdict might have been appealed to a higher military court.

At this point the maître d' appeared beside us with a photographer. Both Raffaele and I reacted as though we'd been ambushed. Seeing the camera, he slouched down in his chair, all but indistinguishable from the shrubbery in the candlelight. The maître d' was pleading with the lawyer to allow "just one picture for the use of the restaurant only." The lawyer looked imploringly at Raffaele, but there was also apprehension in his eyes. Perhaps he was beginning to see—after the movie contract hassle—that he could push his charge just so far. Raffaele was muttering "No, no." I echoed with an emphatic No, then collected my wits and remembered it is always best to smile demurely when saying No to Italian men. I did, and added firmly, "You must allow us some privacy." The maître d' took the rejection gracefully and left with no photograph.

Raffaele looked miserable and was still muttering angrily to himself. At last some of the tension went out of his shoulders, and he looked at me and confessed, "I would have smashed his camera. I would have beat him up. I have a bad temper." He seemed confused at this seizure of emotion; "I'm glad you send them away," he said and sighed.

My own anger subsided as I realized that Raffaele must have been as suspicious of my using him for publicity as I had been of him for courting it. The relief that perhaps we could trust each other in that respect made me laugh as I commented on the absurdity of the situation. Raffaele was surprised at this sudden hilarity, but being essentially good-natured, he joined in. We continued to laugh—astonishing the lawyer, who a moment before had been preparing for trouble.

By the time the evening had ended, my head was spinning with fatigue, but it was hard to sleep when there were so many unanswered questions in my mind. I couldn't help worrying about what would happen to Raffaele, confused and unhappy over the demands of his public image. Even though he had cooked up another perilous journey to flirt with death, I suspected that he wouldn't be allowed to make it. The real question was: At what point does that kind of predilection for death change from a repressed yearning to an active pursuit? When Raffaele discovered that North Vietnam was inaccessible to him, would he turn to some other means of exposing himself as well as others to danger?

One of my questions was answered five months later by a small piece in *The New York Times* of October 15, 1971:

> Remember Raffaele Miniciello? He's the Italian-born former United States marine who hijacked a Trans World Airlines jet in California two years ago and commandeered it to Rome. The 22-year-old Miniciello was released from an Italian prison last spring after serving eighteen months. Now he's gotten his first job, in a Rome restaurant, washing dishes and sorting wine bottles. But he has high hopes for advancement. "I've never been a waiter, but I'll learn," said Miniciello. "The part I like best is being among people. I'm very timid, and this will do me good."

8

WHEN WORD GOT around that I was writing a book about skyjacking, the most common response from people in the airline industry was hostile disapproval. Some of the frustration and anger they feel at their unwilling involvement in this phenomenon apparently transfers itself to anyone who even wants to study the subject. And admittedly, past experience has taught them that when anyone puts the word "skyjack" in print, another skyjacking materializes.

All *they* know is that planes are being ripped off. And as the blood pressure rises with their anger, it acts like cotton batten in the ears. Let some psychiatrist play around with theories about skyjacker pathology, they say. What's the nut's rotten childhood got to do with keeping crews and passengers safe once he goes berserk in the air?

It's a legitimate question. And when they begin to listen to the answers, as some airline officials have, they have to admit that their *responses* to the skyjacker may be one reason why so many skyjackings are successful;

that maybe their ignorance of what motivates him has rendered their decisions hasty and inappropriate.

Certainly there is plenty of evidence now indicating that the airline industry's attitude may have encouraged and even stimulated the crime instead of discouraging it. Such knowledge is a bitter pill to swallow, and, as might be expected, many officials are gagging on the medicine.

Just look at what can be learned from the cases of Sam, George and Gladys, Raffaele. It is of course easier for me to see them as individuals now; to question how well they fit the composite of Dr. Hubbard's typical skyjacker. But to get hung up on the fact that Raffaele and Sam didn't have an alcoholic, violent father, or that George didn't seem to have any paralyzing problems in his relationships with women would be to miss the point of fashioning a valuable if generalizing theory out of psychiatric data.

For example, George and Gladys didn't succeed in getting to Cuba—the crew members on their flight just weren't frightened enough of them. They had their fragile appearance against them, but more importantly the crew talked to George *and listened* to his responses. Using their judgment about what they heard, they correctly decided that George could be talked out of skyjacking.

Sam and Raffaele both had physical appearance in their favor. They in fact fit the news media image of the desperate skyjacker that is fed to crew members as well as to the public. And they each carried a gun, a far more convincing weapon than a kitchen knife or a can of insect spray.

In Sam's case, the crew immediately reacted to him with fear because he was indeed acting crazy. But after a while, when he felt assured of their cooperation, Sam calmed down and became concerned about the passengers and fuel. He told the captain to land in Miami for more fuel if they were running low: to let the passengers off if it would be safer. He wondered if North American Air Defense might harass the plane, creating a dangerous airborne situation. By this time, unfortunately, the crew was no longer really listening to him or they might have perceived that Sam had very mixed feelings about skyjacking to Cuba. He was hastily reassured on all accounts: there was plenty of fuel; the passengers were in no danger; North American Air Defense wouldn't bother them. The crew just wanted to deposit Sam in Cuba as soon as possible—the memory of how crazy and terrifying Sam could be was all too fresh in their minds. Sam then requested a drink, asked the Flight Engineer to hold his gun for him, and relaxed. When he finished his whiskey, the flight engineer politely handed the gun back to him.

Raffaele, of course, actually left *his* gun beside the domestic captain accompanying him and the international flight crew to Rome. He also completely unloaded and stripped down his weapon twice during the flight.

In both of these cases, the skyjacker, after he had been soothed by the crew's cooperative attitude, *disarmed himself*. And in both cases, the crew members could then have taken back control of the airplane and the skyjacker, thus terminating the game.

Why didn't they? Because they were frightened, a normal and realistic reaction under the circumstances.

Imagine your own response if you were terrorized by someone throwing a crazy fit while threatening you with a deadly weapon. When the attacker suddenly becomes docile, even sweet, what are you going to react to—the fact that he's now calm and reasonable, or the memory that he was threatening to kill you a half-hour ago?

With no knowledge of this particular type of aberrant behavior, I for one imagine that I would decide this nut was up to some trick and probably had another weapon hidden on him. I doubt very much that I would have the courage to test him, especially if other people's lives were at stake. I would also remember my airline's instructions—comply with the wishes of the skyjacker. Which is exactly what the crew members on Raffaele's and Sam's flight did, thus adding two more successful skyjackings to the record. And the sensational news coverage of the successes, of course, inspired future skyjackings.

I'm not trying to cast doubt on the courage of the crew members involved. No one had told them anything about skyjackers. Very little research had even been done at the time. The point is, information now available could indeed help crew members play their roles during a skyjacking in such a way as to make a high percentage of skyjackings unsuccessful. They could, for example, look and listen for certain self-defeating moves on the part of the skyjacker that in many cases might allow them to safely defuse the situation and end the drama.

How? Well, that's exactly what happened in the case of Nancy Davis, a new stewardess for Wein Consolidated Airlines in Alaska. In October of 1971 she was completing her last day of training when her instructor mentioned some tapes on crew management of skyjackings, available from the Aberrant Behavior Center (headed by Dr. Hubbard) in Dallas. Nancy asked for the tapes and spent the afternoon listening to them.

The next day she worked her first flight. As she was preparing drinks for her passengers, she turned around in the galley to find a man waving a gun in her face, threatening to shoot her if he wasn't taken to Cuba.

"But this is my first flight," she said incredulously.

The skyjacker was so surprised that he stopped raving and said, "Well, you can tell your grandkids about it."

Nancy sensed in the skyjacker's response a chance to appeal to his better instincts. "Are you going to let me live to have grandchildren?" she asked him. At the same time, she was trying to remember the information on the tapes—keep cool; listen for self-doubts. She told him the gun frightened her, and he put it away. She asked him about his troubles, and he recounted a pathetic list of grievances against society—admitting that he had killed a man for which he had served a prison sentence for manslaughter. Nancy listened sympathetically. When the plane landed for more fuel and to let off the passengers, the skyjacker kindly informed Nancy that she could leave too. She declined his offer, and, as they continued to talk, tried very cautiously to convince him that Cuba might not be the answer to his problems. When the plane landed in Vancouver for more fuel she thought she had won the argument, but he ordered the crew to take off again.

"After we took off, I was really depressed and just sat on my jump seat," she told me. "He was sitting on the floor in front of me. I had been keeping up the bubbly sympathetic act until then. Now that I was quiet he began to look worried, and asked me what the matter was. I said, "You're really going to do it, aren't you?" I shook my head and got up, kind of disgusted, to fix coffee for the crew—without asking his permission. After a few minutes he came over to the galley and started pacing back and forth. "Maybe you're right, maybe things aren't any better in Cuba. Maybe I shouldn't do it." Nancy asked if she should tell the Captain to turn back, and he nodded.

Nancy will be a witness for the defense at the skyjacker's trial. She credits the information on the audio tapes for giving her the confidence to even try to talk an admitted murderer out of skyjacking. The information on those tapes will not and should not be made public knowledge. They do not contain any magic formula for aborting skyjackings; they merely combine up-to-date knowledge of the skyjacker, and crew members' responses to the skyjacker, in such a way that crew members can learn something about their own behavior as well as that of the offender.

Nancy told me something in our interview that points to a less controllable response to skyjacking—the way it gets reported to the public. "When I read about the skyjacking the next day, I wondered if it could be the one I was on. The paper said the skyjacker had demanded to be taken back to Vancouver to get a larger plane for the trip to Cuba. That thought never even occurred to him. He asked us to turn back because he wanted to give up. Where do they get all these distortions?"

Misreporting is, obviously, bad reporting. But what about the sometimes accurate but always detailed reporting that characterizes most news stories about sensational skyjackings? Granted, a skyjacking is an exciting event, a real thriller for those safely on the ground. Everybody loves a thriller. And the news media defends itself with the hallowed phrase "the public's right to know"—lately at the risk of the lives of the passengers and the crew members trying to cope with an explosive situation.

Funny things happen to people's judgment during a crisis. Reporters flock to the scene as airline officials, the FAA, and the control tower are trying to assess the situation through radio contact with the pilot. Radio and television stations interview anyone who'll give out any information. Some airline employee wearing a uniform says, "I think they're going to puncture the tires," and the news goes out as "The tires of the airplane are going to be punctured." Some kid with a short wave radio picks up the control tower conversation with the cockpit, and the reporters move in with their microphones. Everyone is thrilled to hear the rasping conversation of people trying to bargain for their lives.

A false report about a weapons carrier being moved up behind the airplane is broadcast. Somebody says that a bag full of newspapers posing as money is to be delivered. Where did he get this privileged information? Well, he remembered that a couple of years ago this had been done during a skyjacking at Dulles International. Are parachutes being delivered to the airplane? The skyjacker pulls out an article which reported that transmitters are now inserted into the chutes. He informs the crew that he knows what they're up to: he's one of the smart skyjackers who reads the newspapers. He also pulls out a transistor radio and listens to all the false and true—who knows which is which at this point—news reports about weapons carriers and phony FBI crew members and punctured tires; freaks out completely and maybe shoots everyone in sight before he's gunned down. There you have the public's right to know. But what about the crew's and passengers' right to live?

This description is just a composite picture of some but not by any means all of the ways the news media have educated the public to everything they ever wanted to know about skyjacking. The unfortunate fact is that potential skyjackers are *part* of that public. I know reporters who are insulted by any suggestion that the news media have been at best irresponsible in reporting much of the skyjacking news. Some justifiably defend themselves with the fact that they personally have never indulged in this sort of social pornography. They also point out that the sources of most critical information are airline employees. As I said, everybody wants to be a big shot but nobody—not these airline employees nor reporters nor their editors—wants to stop and think, "Do I want to be yet another link in this chain of information that will undoubtedly endanger people's lives?"

It is embarrassing to consider that until recently the only people benefitting from past responses to skyjackings were future skyjackers.

Now, things are changing. Not enough, and not fast enough, but at least in the right direction. Audio and visual tapes on skyjackers' motives and modus operandi are being distributed to the crew members of some airlines—so that for the first time after a decade of skyjacking the people most involved in these sessions of terror will have some idea of what they're up against. So that those airlines who refuse to see the value of these tapes will only have themselves to blame when their uninformed crew members have to play a skyjacking by ear because some management official doesn't hold with psychological mumbo jumbo.

The next bit of good news is that U.S. crew members, sponsored by the Air Line Pilots Association, have formed their own anti-skyjacking organization, T-Plus, to enlist the support of pilot organizations all over the world for speedy ratification of international treaties on skyjacking and sabotage. The "T" stands for treaty, specifically the Tokyo convention, and the "Plus" represents the Hague treaty and any additional treaties that could ensure air safety through international law. The most interesting aspect of this program is the specific intention to accomplish in two years what under normal circumstances might take twenty.

The object of the pilots' campaign is the International Civil Aviation Organization in Montreal. ICAO is the agency responsible for "the *safe* and orderly growth of international civil aviation throughout the world," and the needs of the people of the world for "*safe,* regular, efficient, and economical air transport."

When I first heard about T-Plus I got involved in

helping organize the first attempt to re-educate the public about skyjacking. Assuming that ICAO would welcome help from any quarter in stopping skyjacking, I called their public information officer in October of 1971 to ask about ICAO's role in the kick-off to T-Plus. This was to be a charter flight for the United Nations Ambassadors and skyjacked crew members from New York to Montreal—an event the pilots hoped would focus worldwide attention on skyjacking and, at the same time, pay tribute to ICAO for what they'd done in trying to stop it. (The implication, of course, was that we could all do better.)

I was emphatically informed that the pilots had no business interfering in diplomatic circles, ignoring "proper channels"; that skyjacking was not very high on the agenda of most countries (he named Iceland and Mauritius); that so far as ICAO was concerned the problem was getting just the amount of attention it deserved.

I told him he could hardly expect the pilots and hostesses flying with guns at their heads to agree with him. "You don't understand the complexities of the situation," he said. "Forcing governments on the issue of skyjacking could upset the delicate balance necessary to secure their cooperation on more important treaties." He didn't enlighten me as to what the other treaties were. And at that point I didn't care.

The pilots, perfectly aware of ICAO's attitude, went right on organizing the flight. And ICAO's response was, incredibly, shared by a number of U.S. airlines. The pilots asked an executive of one large airline for the use of a 747 for the UN flight and/or a donation to the cost of the flight. The response? Skyjacking "just wasn't a problem" for their airline.

Ten days later one of their 747's was skyjacked to Cuba, and the plane, crew, and passengers sat for three days while Castro and the U.S. played games. That is what you call instant enlightenment. The executive called back to donate a thousand dollars to the UN flight. He would, it seemed, have given more if the airline hadn't lost so much money on the skyjacking. The pilots, who had chartered a Pan Am 747 by then, refrained from asking him if this airline now had one available.

On November 6, 1971, the T-Plus flight took off from New York with eighty representatives of the United Nations and their wives, and sixty crew members—over thirty of them victims of past skyjackings. Before the luncheon in Montreal, twenty of the skyjacked crew members were introduced to give a brief description of their experiences. Captain Carl Greenwood of National Airlines held the unenviable record of three trips to Havana within one and a half years. There was an understandable note of resignation in his voice as he described his increasing familiarity with madmen in his cockpit.

Captain Robert Wilbur of Eastern did not describe so much as understate his skyjacking. "Are we making our approach?" the skyjacker had asked him. When Captain Wilbur replied that they were, the skyjacker fired; the bullet tore through his arms. First Officer Hartley, who turned to grapple with the skyjacker, was shot in the heart but managed to wound the skyjacker with his own gun before dying. "I then made a routine landing in Boston," concluded Captain Wilbur, who had landed the plane with bullet wounds in both arms and his First Officer dying on the cockpit floor.

Another pilot told of a terrifying gun battle in the sky—wounding the skyjacker, who had killed a passenger. The hostess from that flight who had been caught between the crossfire was unable to make the flight to Montreal—she hadn't quite recovered from the nervous breakdown she suffered after skyjacking.

Captain Dale Hupe of TWA described being forced by a skyjacker to head for Washington, D.C., to pick up a million dollars from President Johnson. Captain Hupe mentioned in passing that he was shot in the stomach by the skyjacker just as FBI agents were about to disarm him.

Captain Jack Priddy of Pan American suggested that the French UN representative and his wife present in the audience could better describe their hasty departure from a 747 with their two babies, seconds before it exploded on the airstrip in Cairo. "This thing has got to stop," he said quietly, indicating with a gesture of his hands the helplessness of any pilot threatened with violence while at the controls of an airplane. The incongruity built into such a situation was eloquently illustrated by the unsensational descriptions delivered by all these skyjacked crew members with an amazing lack of bitterness or theatrics.[1]

The world-wide attention the pilots had hoped to focus on the problems of skyjacking with this flight died with the burial of the story on the transportation pages of the major newspapers around the world. There was an excellent three and a half minutes' reportage of the flight on the NBC nightly news the next day, but CBS had a pro football game going at the time.

The pilots, undaunted, are expanding their T-Plus campaign. But they may have trouble among themselves agreeing on the aims of their campaign if one of my conversations with a skyjacked crew member is any indication of other pilots' opinions. And I'm afraid it is.

I had the disturbing experience of running into Sam the Skyjacker's Captain. After learning that I had interviewed Sam, the Captain proclaimed that skyjackers should be executed—he naturally had Sam in mind. The thrust of his argument was that if skyjackers were executed the whole problem would go away. And even if it didn't, he, at least, would feel better about it. I gave him my argument against the death clause in our skyjacking law, but then undermined it by adding that I didn't believe in the death penalty anyway.

Obviously, what rankled Sam's Captain most was the fact that Sam was free. I asked him if he didn't think Sam was more than a little crazy, and he emphatically agreed. In fact, one source of this Captain's frustration was that he hadn't been allowed to describe just how crazy and frightening Sam had been, because the prosecution was trying to prove that Sam was just drunk. "You interview and make a celebrity of this guy," the Captain fumed. "Why don't you ask us how it is with a nut in the cockpit threatening to kill us any minute while we're trying to fly a plane safely?"

There just didn't seem to be any way to convince him that keeping nuts out of the cockpit was precisely my concern—as opposed to killing nuts, which seemed to be his. I recalled something that Sam and his wife had told me on one of their trips to New York for a television interview. "Janey [their oldest daughter] just wrote a theme on capital punishment," Sam said proudly. "She's for it in certain cases," said Carolyn. Not in Daddy's case, I assumed. It occurred to me that Sam and this Captain would probably have more grounds for agreement on the subject of crime and punishment than I had with either of them.

Many people—particularly airline people—will be disturbed by much of my criticism of governmental and air industry response to the threat of skyjacking. Those same people will feel that I am being unfairly negative about some sincere efforts to cope with the problem. So I would like to retreat to the one point on which we all *do* agree: the inevitability, despite all the present deterrence programs, of a major air disaster during a skyjacking.

Unless the present climate of vulnerability is removed through international cooperation, a disaster is as inevitable as were those skyjacking-provoked tragedies which have already resulted in loss of life and aircraft. It was only miraculously quick action which prevented the passengers and crew members from being blown up with the Pan Am 747 at Cairo in September of 1970. Imagine your response if you heard that a 747 with, say, 362 passengers and 14 crew members had crashed or exploded through the ineptitude or homicidal-suicidal determination of a skyjacker? Horror, fear, anger. And helplessness? Because with all the warnings and forecasts of the inevitable, nothing effective was done to prevent it?

I wonder if, after such a disaster, all nations would *then* find it expedient as well as morally imperative to assume their responsibilities by drafting enforceable anti-skyjacking laws. It's possible. But it's also possible that if these regulatory agencies simply proceed at their own speed, as they seem determined to do despite the pilots and T-Plus, it could take more than one disaster to drive the point home.

I would prefer not to wait for disaster-inspired action in any case. To quote from a speech by President Nixon after the economic and psychological disaster of the PLFP skyjackings in September of 1970:

> . . . Additional action is necessary. It should include . . . international agreements to suspend air service to countries which refuse to cooperate in the release of hijacked aircraft and the punishment of hijackers.

To date, the representatives of ICAO have not put such sanctions into any of their already inadequate anti-skyjacking treaties. The members of the International Federation of Airline Pilots Association vacillate about taking aggressive action on this issue—the pilots feel that it is ICAO's responsibility as the lawmaking body for international civil aviation to provide laws ensuring the safety of passengers and crews.

What has been happening while they wait for ICAO to act? In the years since the Palestinian skyjackings, three crew members have been killed, four wounded; two passengers killed and fifteen wounded; one aircraft blown up and three damaged by explosives—all because of skyjackers. These incidents took place on the airlines of Korea, India, Russia, the United States, Iran, and Cuba. Over the past twenty-three years, skyjacking-provoked fatalities and injuries also occurred on the airlines of Bulgaria, Ecuador, Chile, Israel, and Czechoslovakia.

I would think that, politics aside, the crew members of these countries collectively might express some loud displeasure about the continuing lack of provision for their safety. That they might show some of the courage they have displayed during skyjackings to present an ultimatum to ICAO demanding enforceable anti-skyjacking laws—along with the explicit warning that the international fraternity of crew members itself has the power to impose sanctions if the designated governing body won't do it for them. That pilots might refuse to fly to any country that refused to act responsibly.

As for the press? Suppose we looked at it this way. In the days when the kidnapping of a single child or adult was front page news, the FBI and the police and responsible reporters tried to keep out of print anything that would endanger the life of the victim. Human nature being what it is, there was the occasional reporter who couldn't keep quiet even if it did mean endangering the kidnapped person's life. The issue wasn't a free press, it was plain human responsibility.

Well, skyjacking involves the kidnapping of anywhere from a few to a few hundred people under extraordinarily hazardous circumstances. In the old days, a kidnapper might deliberately kill his victim before or after getting his ransom. Today, in an airplane, the kidnapper—homicidal or not—may be toying with factors beyond his control. The only thing keeping that plane up in the air is the skill and attention of two pilots. Those pilots don't have to be killed or wounded to create a lethal hazard; a crucial distraction could do it. Another airplane could do it. Or, a deranged skyjacker could try to force a landing at an airport which cannot accommodate a plane of that size or force a take-off with inadequate fuel or maintenance. And while sudden depressurizing of a plane's cabin from a bullet hole is not likely, think what would happen if a grenade went off—even if it was dropped down a toilet in time.

A conventional kidnapping involves worried parents or harried police or FBI men; an aerial kidnapping can involve hundreds of distraught persons in the air and on the ground, any one of whom could do something that would make a skyjacker lose control. But there are newspapermen and radio and television reporters who might not dream of endangering the life of the victim in a ground kidnapping, who endanger a whole planeload of people during a kidnapping in the sky. If skyjacking is to be stopped, foreign countries ought to send skyjackers back to the country of departure—and news media editors ought to send reporters who've endangered human lives back to journalism school instead of commending them for a scoop.

Crew members may not be getting combat pay, but in the skyjacking war they're always out on patrol. There are those who are trying through T-Plus to involve the public in an anti-skyjacking campaign, but the news media haven't been helping on that front, either. So far, the T-Plus efforts have earned about as much news coverage and public response to crew members' plights as the Palestinians got *before* they started blowing up airplanes.

What do the crew members have to do to get some action, gentlemen? Skyjack the United States Senate?

On February 21, 1972, Palestinian guerrillas skyjacked a Frankfurt-bound Lufthansa jet, en route from New Delhi, and forced it to land in Yemen. The sensational news that Robert Kennedy, Jr., was one of the passengers was followed by the equally sensational report that Lufthansa officials had paid $5,000,000 ransom for the lives of the crew and the return of their airplane in one piece. Blow by blow descriptions of the skyjacking made front-page news around the world.

On the morning of March 7, 1972, Trans World Airlines received a phone call instructing them to go to a locker at their JFK terminal—where they found a demand for two million dollars, along with the assurance that planes would be blown up unless the ransom was paid. (At that moment, in fact, a flight bound for Los Angeles was carrying a bomb.) The plane returned to JFK, and a German Shepherd named Brandy sniffed out the device in the cockpit. It was defused twelve minutes before it was set to explode.

The next morning a TWA 707 exploded at the Las Vegas airport. The plane allegedly had been thoroughly searched. The bomb, it turned out, had been planted in the first aid kit.

On March 9, I worked a flight to London. During

the pre-flight briefing we received an instruction which topped "Throw any grenades into the lavatory." It was: "Check all the first aid kits for bombs."

Boarding the plane, I headed straight for the first aid kit, at which point it suddenly seemed logical to wonder what I would do if I *found* a bomb.

What was it Raffaelle had said about Vietnam? "They treat me like cannon fodder. Always when we go on patrol, they say 'Send the Wop in front with the mine sweeper.'" At least Raffaelle had a mine sweeper.

Just to see how far this insanity had affected our procedures, I asked a captain what a hostess should do upon finding a bomb in the first aid kit. "Well," he said, "if it doesn't detonate when you open the kit, put it down very gently and runlikehell."

What does it all mean, please? Why did those Lufthansa officials pay the $5,000,000 ransom? Why did the news media tell every lunatic in the world how easy it is to rip off the airlines? Did the TWA employee who tipped off the press about the bomb and extortion plot get paid the usual $20?

We have advertised our vulnerability, our inability to act in international concert, and, now, we are forced to defuse bombs because we didn't defuse the situation long ago by making extortion and skyjacking crimes which don't pay.

Because skyjackers have proved that both crimes *do* pay, we are now faced with some ghastly choices:

We can negotiate enforceable international agreements making the payment of ransom and/or the harboring of skyjackers a crime punishable by the grounding of all air traffic to the offending country, *and* suffer the interim period during which planes will undoubtedly be blown up and lives be lost—until the lunatics get the point that the game is over.

Or we can let the situation continue as is, with each country and airline carrying out different policies protesting short-term interests, *and* suffer the same consequences—planes being blown up and lives being lost—for an indefinite period.

The airplane as an autonomous political unit with the captain as king has now become a police state. Its borders are patrolled by men bristling with guns and detection devices. The mutual trust that airline employees always took for granted is no longer assumed. What is in the box that mechanic is carrying into the cockpit? Is that uniformed man coming up the ramp really the captain?

I ask myself if I want to go on wondering what the next crisis will be. Will I be told to check for bombs in the coffee pot, while the airlines are paying off some crackpot so he'll tell them where the bombs are? Will the bombs go off anyway? How would I feel as the hostage of a skyjacker who is threatening to blow up me and the plane unless money or prisoners are delivered? If there's a chance for me to be sent up in smoke, does it make any difference whether it's a stupid, senseless death or whether there is a reason for it? At this point, with my feet safely on terra firma, I think there is a difference. I am willing to sign a petition demanding laws saying "NO ransom, no bargains, no sanctuary."

With those laws in force, if some lunatic does put them to the ultimate test by taking my plane along when he says "Goodbye cruel world," at least the unhappy ending would have some meaning. As it stands now, we are all just potential cannon fodder, nervously eyeing the first-aid box.

Appendix I Averted and Incomplete Hijacking Attempts

DATE	
7/31/61	Subdued by co-pilot and passengers prior to take-off after shooting pilot and passenger agent; also shot at passengers.
8/3/61 Incomplete	Border Patrol Officers shot out tires and engines prior to take-off; hijackers were eventually disarmed.
10/11/65	Captain used flare pistol to disarm one man; a ramp agent using a shotgun apprehended the second man; aircraft not in flight.
10/26/65	Captain knocked gun from hijacker with fire axe (during flight). Captain and Flight Engineer subdued individual.
11/17/65	Sixteen-year-old high school student after firing nine shots was disarmed and subdued by crew; aircraft was in flight.
2/9/68	Details not known. Marine Private attempted to hijack Pan Am flight from Saigon to Hong Kong; aircraft did not depart.
7/4/68	Convict in custody of U.S. Marshals threatened stewardess and ordered pilot to fly to Mexico;

DATE	
	pilot pretended compliance but landed at Las Vegas, Nevada.
7/12/68 Incomplete	Flight crew engaged gunman in conversation; persuaded him to give up hijacking attempt.
11/2/68	Co-pilot diverted gunman's attention; Captain wrested shotgun from would-be hijacker; aircraft not in flight.
1/13/69	Stewardess ran into the cockpit and locked the door after being confronted by a hijacker with a shotgun. Plane was on final approach and landing was completed. Hijacker was taken into custody while sitting quietly in his seat with the unloaded shotgun at his feet.
2/3/69	Crew convinced 21-year-old hijacker and his 18-year-old female accomplice that refueling was necessary at Miami. Flight originated in New York. Ground crew became suspicious at Miami and alerted police. Pilot persuaded very sensitive and disturbed hijacker to relinquish the knife and aerosol spray–type can which he was carrying.
3/19/69 Incomplete	Hijacker was convinced of the necessity for refueling in New Orleans. While on the ground, he was persuaded to allow passengers to deplane. An FBI Special Agent (passenger) wrestled the gun from the hijacker and placed him under arrest. One shot was fired from the hijacker's gun, but no injuries resulted.
5/30/69	Two prisoners who were being transported by law enforcement officers handed a note to the stewardess indicating that they had a hand grenade, and unless the plane was flown to Cuba, they would explode the grenade. The aircraft was on final approach and the pilot landed without incident. The prisoners were taken off the plane after

DATE	
	landing by law enforcement officers. The prisoners did not have a hand grenade or any other type of weapon.
8/5/69	Seventy-four-year-old man attempt to hijack aircraft while in flight. He was armed with a five-inch straight razor and a pocketknife. Pilot convinced him refueling was necessary in order to fly to Cuba. Hijacker commented he would be apprehended if a refueling stop was necessary and returned to his seat. He was taken into custody at original destination.
9/10/69	Subject grabbed a stewardess and said, "I want to go to Cuba." He returned to his seat after failing to unlock the cockpit door with keys provided by the stewardess. He was then subdued by passengers and taken into custody at San Juan.
11/10/69	Fourteen-year-old boy boarded aircraft without ticket using an 18-year-old girl as a hostage. He held a butcher knife against the girl's back and demanded to be taken to Sweden. When told the plane was not capable of such a long flight (DC-9) he requested it be flown to Mexico. The youth was persuaded to surrender as the plane taxied about the runways.
1/6/70	A male passenger, armed with a knife, attempted to hijack the aircraft while holding a stewardess as a hostage. The incident occurred shortly before a scheduled landing. The hijacker lost his balance, after the landing, when the pilot made a tight turn and reversed the engines. The hijacker was overpowered by passengers and crew members.
3/17/70 Incomplete	Armed male entered cockpit and demanded that aircraft be flown out to sea. Stated he wanted to be notified when only 2 minutes of fuel remained. When captain turned aircraft in the direction of

DATE	
	U.S. mainland, hijacker began shooting at the Captain and Co-pilot. Co-pilot, although mortally wounded, succeeded in shooting the hijacker twice with hijacker's revolver. Captain who had been shot in both arms landed plane at original destination. Hijacker recovered.
4/23/70	An armed male adult hijacked a bus and forced the driver to take him to the airport. He then proceeded to use the driver as a hostage, as he boarded an air carrier aircraft which was boarding passengers. Michigan State Police overpowered the individual after responding to a call for assistance from the crew.
6/4/70 Incomplete	Gun-wielding male entered cockpit and demanded to be flown to Washington, D.C., and that 100 thousand dollars be ready and fuel truck meet the aircraft upon landing at Dulles Airport. Later further requested that an internationally qualified pilot also meet the aircraft at Dulles. The aircraft landed at Dulles. The new pilot picked up the bag of money ($100,000) and boarded the hijacked aircraft. It took off and flew around with no destination imposed by the hijacker, who was dissatisfied with the amount of money. The aircraft returned to Dulles to supposedly pick up more money. Fake money bags had been placed on the landing field. As the aircraft rolled to a stop, its tires were shot out. Vehicles blocked any further movement of the aircraft. The passengers deplaned via emergency doors and chutes. The FBI and crew overpowered and captured the hijacker in the process of which the hijacker was wounded slightly and the original pilot was wounded in the abdomen.
8/3/70	Male armed with starter pistol shouted to stewardess to have aircraft diverted from Munich/West Berlin to Budapest. Pilot dissuaded him

DATE	
	from hijacking aircraft. Met by police as he deplaned at Berlin.
9/15/70 Incomplete	Hijacker armed with pistol handed a note to the chief stewardess stating he wished to go to North Korea. Hijacker remained in his seat. Aircraft landed at San Francisco for refueling at which time 35 women, children, and military were allowed to evacuate. Hijacker was then shot by a Brinks guard who had been a passenger on the aircraft.
9/22/70	A Federal prisoner, who was being transported from Boston, Massachusetts to San Juan, P.R., locked himself in lavatory and threatened to burn airplane if plane was not diverted to his destination of choice. He was overpowered and forcibly subdued by two escorting U.S. Marshals.
12/19/70 Incomplete	Hijacker handed a note to a stewardess stating that he had a gun and directing flight to Cuba. Hijacker permitted landing at Tulsa to allow passengers to deplane. Crew deplaned with the passengers, stranding the hijacker in the aircraft. Police boarded the aircraft and arrested the unarmed hijacker who was hiding in a washroom.
12/21/70 Incomplete	Hijacker stated he had bomb and wanted to go to Mexico. Crew convinced him of necessity to return to San Juan (point of departure) to refuel. Hijacker was overpowered by the crew after landing at San Juan.
3/8/71 Incomplete	Hijacker armed with .38 cal. pistol. Initiated hijack attempt while aircraft on ground loading for departure to New Orleans. Other passengers deplaned and flight departed for Montreal, Canada. When in vicinity of Knoxville, Tenn., crew persuaded hijacker to abandon hijack attempt and divert to Miami. FBI agents surrounded the air-

DATE	
	craft as it stopped on the ramp and took the hijacker into custody.
3/31/71	Fourteen-year-old hijacker enplaned without ticket at Birmingham airport. Armed with pistol, held hostess as hostage. Demanded to go to Cuba. Allowed passengers and other hostesses to deplane. Hostess convinced him to abandon the hijacking.
4/21/71	Hijacker searched prior to boarding. Prior to arrival at Miami, hijacker claimed he had a gun and grenade, would permit aircraft to land Miami, but wanted to go to Italy. Pilot called bluff. Aircraft landed Miami. Hijacker arrested. He carried no weapons.
5/28/71 Incomplete	Hijacker who boarded at Miami threatened stewardess with fake acid, threatened to blow up aircraft with fake explosives, ordered the aircraft to fly to LaGuardia Airport, N.Y. (original destination), and that his wife and son be at the airport. Upon arrival he permitted the passengers and stewardesses to deplane. His wife and son did not arrive. After 1½ hours the hijacker ordered the plane to take off. Once aloft he demanded to be flown to Nassau, that ½ million dollars be placed on the runway there and that he be met by the N.Y. representative of the Irish Republican Army. Upon deplaning in Nassau, the hijacker was captured.
6/4/71 Incomplete	Hijacker armed with pistol commandeered aircraft 10 minutes after takeoff and demanded to be flown to Israel. When told the aircraft did not have enough fuel for trip, hijacker allowed landing at Dulles and permitted passengers and stewardesses to deplane. After 3 hours on the ground, hijacker went to get a drink of water leaving pistol on seat. Hijacker taken into custody.

DATE	
6/12/71 Incomplete	Twenty-three-year-old Negro, armed with pistol, forced his way on board aircraft, held stewardess hostage and demanded to be flown to North Vietnam. He killed one passenger who got in the way, then allowed passengers, bodyguard and hostess (except hostage) to deplane. During this pause, a deputy U.S. Marshal sneaked aboard the aircraft. The aircraft then took off for New York, ostensibly to change to an aircraft with longer range. During the flight, several shots were exchanged between the crew, marshal and hijacker. When plane landed at JFK, the crew and marshal escaped. The hijacker was wounded and captured by the FBI.
6/18/71	Hijacker boarded aircraft after termination of flight. Claimed to have explosive and acid. Demanded to go to Cuba. Captain informed would-be hijacker that aircraft needed fuel and additional crew. While second pilot was enplaning, he overpowered hijacker.
7/2-3/71 Incomplete	Hijacker boarded at Mexico City accompanied by girlfriend. Near San Antonio he passed a note to the pilot threatening harm unless his demands were met. He diverted the flight to Monterrey, Mexico, to pick up $100,000 he extorted from the airline. There he allowed the passengers to deplane. He then, over the next 24 hours, directed the plane to Lima (Peru), Rio de Janeiro (Brazil), and Buenos Aires (Argentina), seeking an Algerian representative to arrange political asylum. He surrendered to authorities at Buenos Aires.
7/23/71 Incomplete	Hijacker held stewardess as hostage and demanded to be flown to Milan, Italy. Crew informed him that aircraft did not have the necessary range and convinced him to return to origin to switch to longer-range aircraft. While waiting

DATE	
	to board new aircraft, hijacker was shot and killed by FBI.
9/3/71	Hijacker threatened stewardess with ice pick and demanded to be flown to Cuba. Dead heading crew sensed something amiss, intervened, and with passenger assistance, overpowered hijacker.
9/24/71	Hijacker, armed with pistol and high explosives, planned to threaten to blow up aircraft to effect the release of two Black Panthers from prison and then fly them to Algeria in hijacked aircraft. Authorities tipped off. Passengers, including hijacker, deplaned prior to takeoff under pretext of mechanical difficulties. Hijacker apprehended in terminal following threat to shoot arresting officer and to blow up explosives.
10/4/71 Incomplete	Chartered aircraft en route Nashville-Atlanta diverted by 2 armed men to Jacksonville for refuel and supplies and further flight to Bahamas. FBI agent shot out tires at Jacksonville. One hijacker, his wife and pilot killed. Co-pilot safe. One hijacker captured.
10/18/71 Incomplete	Scheduled B-737 flight from Anchorage to Bethel, Alaska, was hijacked by a lone armed man shortly after departure. The stewardess convinced the hijacker to return to Anchorage to discharge the passengers. The hijacker then ordered the flight to Vancouver, B.C., where the aircraft was refueled for an onward flight to Mexico City and Cuba. An hour or so out of Vancouver, B.C., the hijacker ordered the aircraft to return in order to switch to a larger aircraft. A Royal Canadian Mounted Police inspector boarded the B-737 when it landed. An hour later, the hijacker permitted the crew to deplane, and he surrendered to the RCMP.

DATE	
12/24/71 Incomplete	Scheduled B-707 flight from Minneapolis/St. Paul to Chicago was hijacked by a lone armed man shortly after departure. He fired revolver shots into the bulkhead and ordered the stewardess to inform the captain that he had just killed a man and that he wanted $300,000 ransom. The flight landed at Chicago and the money was delivered. The hijacker allowed all but two passengers to deplane. While the hijacker was counting the money, the cockpit crew escaped. While the hijacker went to the lavatory, one of the three stewardesses escaped. The aircraft was surrounded and spot-lighted. The two remaining stewardesses and one of the passengers jumped from the aircraft. The hijacker then threw out the money and surrendered.
12/26/71 Unsuccessful	Scheduled B-707 flight from Chicago to San Francisco diverted to Salt Lake City when intoxicated male brandished a plastic replica of a pistol. Hijacker stated he had a pressure type bomb on his person set to explode if aircraft descended through 2,500 feet. He was subdued by a stewardess and a passenger. Personal effects and statements made following his arrest indicated that he wanted to prove that any person could hijack an air carrier.

Appendix II Kinds of Weapons Involved in Hijacking Incidents

TYPE	NUMBER OF INCIDENTS *
Firearms (Alleged and Real)	87
BB Gun	1
Knives	21
Bombs, Explosives (Alleged and Real)	35
Razor or Razor Blade	3
Tear Gas Pen	1
Broken Bottle	1
Fire Threat	1
Hatchet	1
Acid	1
Ice Pick	1

UPDATED: 1 January 1972

FEDERAL AVIATION ADMINISTRATION
OFFICE OF AIR TRANSPORTATION SECURITY

* Several hijackers used combinations of two or more weapons.

Appendix III Master List of Skyjacking Attempts Through Worldwide, Air Carrier, and General Aviation

ıe list is compiled from the files of the Federal Aviation Administration, e Department of State, International Air Transport Association; as well newspaper and magazine files. The list does not include theft of aircraft the skyjacking of military aircraft. Successful attempts are indicated an asterisk following the skyjacking attempt number.

ttempt No.	*Date*	*Country Owning Aircraft*	*Departure/Arrival*
1*	(1930)	Peru	Peru/Peru
2*	7/25/47	Rumania	Rumania/Turkey
3*	4/8/48	Czechoslovakia	Czechoslovakia/US Zone Germany
4*	5/4/48	Czechoslovakia	Czechoslovakia/US Zone Germany
5*	6/4/48	Yugoslavia	Yugoslavia/Italy
6*	6/17/48	Rumania	Rumania/Austria
7*	6/30/48	Bulgaria	Bulgaria/Turkey
8	7/16/48	Hong Kong	Hong Kong/Unknown
9*	9/12/48	Greece	Greece/Yugoslavia
10*	4/29/49	Rumania	Rumania/Greece
11*	12/9/49	Rumania	Rumania/Yugoslavia
12*	12/16/49	Poland	Poland/Denmark
13*	3/24/50	Czechoslovakia	Czechoslovakia/US Zone Germany
14*	3/24/50	Czechoslovakia	Czechoslovakia/US Zone Germany
15*	3/24/50	Czechoslovakia	Czechoslovakia/US Zone Germany
16	12/30/52	Philippines	Philippines/Red China

Attempt No.	*Date*	*Country Owning Aircraft*	*Departure/Arrival*
17*	3/23/53	Czechoslovakia	Czechoslovakia/West Germany
18*	2/16/58	South Korea	South Korea/North Korea
19	4/10/58	South Korea	South Korea/North Korea
20*	10/22/58	Cuba	Cuba/Cuba
21	11/1/58	Cuba	Cuba/Cuba
22*	11/6/58	Cuba	Cuba/Cuba
23*	4/16/59	Cuba	Cuba/USA
24*	4/10/59	Haiti	Haiti/Cuba
25*	10/2/59	Cuba	Cuba/USA
26*	4/12/60	Cuba	Cuba/USA
27*	7/5/60	Cuba	Cuba/USA
28*	7/18/60	Cuba	Cuba/Jamaica
29	7/19/60	Australia	Australia/Singapore
30*	7/28/60	Cuba	Cuba/USA
31	8/21/60	USSR	USSR/Unknown
32*	10/29/60	Cuba	Cuba/USA
33	12/8/60	Cuba	Cuba/USA
34*	5/1/61	USA	USA/Cuba NAL
35*	7/3/61	Cuba	Cuba/USA
36*	7/24/61	USA	USA/Cuba EAL
37	7/31/61	USA	USA/USA PAC
38	8/3/61	USA	USA/Cuba CAL
39*	8/9/61	USA	USA/Cuba PAA
40	8/9/61	Cuba	Cuba/USA
41	9/10/61	USSR	USSR/Armenia
42*	11/10/61	Portugal	Portugal/Spanish Morocco
43*	11/27/61	Venezuela	Venezuela/Netherlands Antilles
44	3/17/62	France	France/France
45*	4/13/62	USA	USA/Cuba
46	4/16/62	Netherlands	Netherlands/East Germany
47	8/5/63	USA	USA/Cuba
48*	11/28/63	Venezuela	Venezuela/Trinidad
49*	2/18/64	USA	USA/Cuba
50	10/19/64	USSR	USSR/Unknown
51	Sp '65	USSR	USSR/Unknown
52*	8/31/65	USA	USA/USA HAW AL
53	10/11/65	USA	USA/USA ALOHA AL

Attempt No.	Date	Country Owning Aircraft	Departure/Arrival
54	10/26/65	USA	USA/Cuba NAL
55	11/17/65	USA	USA/Cuba NAL
56	3/27/66	Cuba	Cuba/USA
57	Sp '66	USSR	USSR/Turkey
58*	7/7/66	Cuba	Cuba/Jamaica
59	8/9/66	USSR	USSR/Turkey
60*	9/28/66	Argentina	Argentina/Falkland Islands
61*	2/7/67	Egypt	Egypt/Jordan
62*	4/23/67	Nigeria	Nigeria/Nigeria
63*	6/30/67	U.K.	United Kingdom/Algeria
64*	8/6/67	Colombia	Colombia/Cuba
65*	9/9/67	Colombia	Colombia/Cuba
66*	11/20/67	USA	USA/Cuba
67	2/9/68	USA	USA/Hong Kong PAA
68*	2/17/68	USA	USA/Cuba
69*	2/21/68	USA	USA/Cuba Delta
70*	3/5/68	Colombia	Colombia/Cuba
71*	3/12/68	USA	USA/Cuba NAL
72*	3/16/68	Mexico	Mexico/Cuba
73*	3/22/68	Venezuela	Venezuela/Cuba
74*	6/19/68	Venezuela	Venezuela/Cuba
75*	6/29/68	USA	USA/Cuba Southeast AL
76*	7/1/68	USA	USA/Cuba NW
77	7/4/68	USA	USA/Mexico TWA
78*	7/12/68	USA	USA/Cuba
79	7/12/68	USA	USA/Cuba Delta
80*	7/17/68	USA	USA/Cuba NAL
81*	7/23/68	Israel	Israel/Algeria
82*	8/4/68	USA	USA/Cuba
83*	8/22/68	USA	USA/Cuba
84	9/11/68	Canada	Canada/Cuba
85*	9/20/68	USA	USA/Cuba EAL
86*	9/22/68	Colombia	Colombia/Cuba
87*	9/22/68	Colombia	Colombia/Cuba
88*	10/6/68	Mexico	Mexico/Cuba
89*	10/23/68	USA	USA/Cuba
90*	10/30/68	Mexico	Mexico/USA

Attempt No.	*Date*	*Country Owning Aircraft*	*Departure/Arrival*
91	11/2/68	USA	USA/Cuba EAL
92*	11/4/68	USA	USA/Cuba NAL
93*	11/6/68	Philippines	Philippines/Philippines
94*	11/8/68	Greece	Greece/Greece
95*	11/18/68	Mexico	Mexico/Cuba
96*	11/23/68	USA	USA/Cuba EAL
97*	11/24/68	USA	USA/Cuba PAA
98*	11/30/68	USA	USA/Cuba EAL
99*	12/3/68	USA	USA/Cuba NAL
100*	12/11/68	USA	USA/Cuba TWA
101*	12/11/68	USA	USA/Cuba EAL
102*	1/2/69	USA	USA/Cuba EAL
103*	1/2/69	Greece	Greece/Egypt
104*	1/7/69	Colombia	Colombia/Cuba
105*	1/9/69	USA	USA/Cuba EAL
106*	1/11/69	USA	USA/Cuba UAL
107*	1/11/69	Peru	Peru/Cuba
108	1/13/69	USA	USA/Cuba Delta
109*	1/19/69	USA	USA/Cuba EAL
110*	1/19/69	Ecuador	Ecuador/Cuba
111*	1/24/69	USA	USA/Cuba NAL
112*	1/28/69	USA	USA/Cuba NAL
113*	1/28/69	USA	USA/Cuba EAL
114*	1/31/69	USA	USA/Cuba NAL
115*	2/3/69	USA	USA/Cuba EAL
116	2/3/69	USA	USA/Cuba NAL
117*	2/5/69	Colombia	Colombia/Cuba
118	2/8/69	Mexico	Mexico/Cuba
119*	2/10/69	USA	USA/Cuba EAL
120*	2/11/69	Venezuela	Venezuela/Cuba
121*	2/25/69	USA	USA/Cuba EAL
122*	3/5/69	USA	USA/Cuba NAL
123	3/11/69	Colombia	Colombia/Cuba
124*	3/15/69	Colombia	Colombia/Cuba
125*	3/17/69	Peru	Peru/Cuba
126*	3/17/69	USA	USA/Cuba Delta
127	3/19/69	USA	USA/Cuba Delta

empt o.	*Date*	*Country Owning Aircraft*	*Departure/Arrival*
28*	3/25/69	USA	USA/Cuba Delta
29*	4/11/69	Ecuador	Ecuador/Cuba
30*	4/13/69	USA	USA/Cuba PAA
31*	4/14/69	Colombia	Colombia/Cuba
32 [1]			
33*	5/5/69	USA	USA/Cuba NAL
34*	5/20/69	Colombia	Colombia/Cuba
35*	5/26/69	USA	USA/Cuba NE
36	5/30/69	USA	USA/Cuba Tex. Int.
37*	6/4/69	Portugal	Portugal/Congo
38*	6/17/69	USA	USA/Cuba TWA
39*	6/20/69	Colombia	Colombia/Cuba
40*	6/22/69	USA	USA/Cuba EAL
41*	6/25/69	USA	USA/Cuba UAL
42*	6/28/69	USA	USA/Cuba EAL
43*	7/3/69	Ecuador	Ecuador/Cuba
44	7/10/69	Colombia	Colombia/Cuba
45*	7/26/69	USA	USA/Cuba CAL
46*	7/26/69	Mexico	Mexico/Cuba
47	7/29/69	Mexico	Nicaragua/Cuba
48*	7/31/69	USA	USA/Cuba TWA
49*	8/4/69	Colombia	Colombia/Cuba
50	8/5/69	USA	USA/Cuba EAL
51*	8/12/69	Ethiopia	Ethiopia/Sudan
52*	8/14/69	USA	USA/Cuba NE
53*	8/16/69	Greece	Greece/Albania
54*	8/18/69	Egypt	Egypt/Saudi Arabia
55*	8/23/69	Colombia	Colombia/Cuba
56*	8/29/69	USA	USA/Cuba NAL
57*	8/29/69	USA	USA/Syria TWA
58*	9/6/69	Ecuador	Ecuador/Cuba
59	9/6/69	Ecuador	Ecuador/Cuba
60*	9/7/69	USA	USA/Cuba EAL
61	9/10/69	USA	USA/Cuba EAL
62*	9/13/69	Ethiopia	Ethiopia/S. Yemen Republic

1. On 5/3/69 prosecution was declined because of insufficient evidence. has been determined not to be an offense covered by the Air Piracy Act.

Attempt No.	Date	Country Owning Aircraft	Departure/Arrival
163*	9/13/69	Honduras	Honduras/San Salvador
164*	9/16/69	Turkey	Turkey/Bulgaria
165*	9/24/69	USA	USA/Cuba NAL
166*	10/8/69	Brazil	Brazil/Cuba
167*	10/8/69	Argentina	Argentina/Cuba
168*	10/9/69	USA	USA/Cuba NAL
169*	10/19/69	Poland	Poland/W. Berlin (French)
170*	10/21/69	USA	USA/Cuba (Mex. C.-Merida) PAA
171*	10/28/69	Colombia	Colombia/Cuba
172*	10/31/69	USA	USA/Italy (Rome) TWA
173*	11/4/69	Nicaragua	Nicaragua/Cuba
174*	11/4/69	Brazil	Brazil/Cuba
175	11/8/69	Argentina	Argentina/Cuba
176	11/10/69	USA	USA/(Sweden, Mexico or Brazi DL
177	11/12/69	Chile	Chile/Cuba
178*	11/12/69	Brazil	Brazil/Cuba
179*	11/13/69	Colombia	Colombia/Cuba
180*	11/18/69	Mexico	Mexico/Cuba
181*	11/20/69	Poland	Poland/Austria
182*	11/31/69	Brazil	Brazil/Cuba
183*	12/2/69	USA	USA/Cuba TWA
184*	12/11/69	South Korea	Korea/N. Korea
185	12/13/69	Ethiopia	Ethiopia/Yemen
186	12/19/69	Chile	Chile/Cuba
187*	12/23/69	Costa Rica	Costa Rica/Cuba
188*	12/26/69	USA	USA/Cuba UAL
189	Dec. '69	Ethiopia	Ethiopia/unknown
190*	1/1/70	Brazil	Brazil/Cuba
191	1/6/70	USA	USA/Switzerland DL
192	1/7/70	Spain	Spain/Albania
193*	1/8/70	USA	USA/Lebanon TWA
194	1/9/70	Panama	Panama/Cuba
195*	1/24/70	Curacao	Netherlands Antilles/Cuba
196	2/6/70	Chile	Chile/Cuba
197	2/10/70	Israel	Israel/Libya
198*	2/16/70	USA	USA/Cuba EA

empt No.	*Date*	*Country Owning Aircraft*	*Departure/Arrival*
99	3/10/70	E. Germany	E. Germany/Unknown
00*	3/11/70	USA	USA/Cuba UN
01*	3/11/70	Colombia	Colombia/Cuba
02*	3/12/70	Brazil	Chile/Cuba
03	3/17/70	USA	USA/Indefinite EA
04*	3/24/70	Argentina	Argentina/Cuba
05*	3/25/70	British Honduras	British Honduras/Cuba
06*	3/30/70	Japan	Japan/N. Korea
07	4/22/70	USA	USA/Indefinite N. Central
08*	4/22/70	USA	USA/Cuba
09*	4/25/70	Brazil	Brazil/Cuba
10	5/1/70	Trinidad	Trinidad/Algeria (landed Havana)
11*	5/5/70	Czechoslovakia	Czechoslovakia/Austria
12*	5/12/70	Curacao	Curacao/Cuba
13	5/14/70	Australia	Australia/Unknown
14*	5/14/70	Brazil	Brazil/Cuba
15*	5/21/70	Colombia	Colombia/Cuba
16*	5/24/70	Mexico	Mexico/Cuba
17*	5/25/70	USA	USA/Cuba DL
18*	5/25/70	USA	USA/Cuba AA
19*	5/30/70	Italy	Italy/Egypt
20*	5/31/70	Colombia	Colombia/Cuba
21	6/4/70	USA	USA/Indefinite [2] TWA
22	6/5/70	Poland	Poland/Copenhagen
23*	6/8/70	Czechoslovakia	Czechoslovakia/W. Germany
24	6/9/70	Poland	Poland/Austria
25	6/21/70	Iran	Iran/Iraq
26*	6/22/70	USA	USA/Egypt PAA
227*	6/26/70	Venezuela	Venezuela/Colombia
228*	7/1/70	USA	USA/Cuba NAL
229	7/1/70	Brazil	Brazil/Cuba
230*	7/4/70	Brazil	Brazil/Cuba
231*	7/11/70	Saudi Arabia	Saudi Arabia/Syria

2. There did not appear to be any particular location to which the aircraft s being diverted.

Attempt No.	*Date*	*Country Owning Aircraft*	*Departure/Arrival*
232	7/22/70	South Vietnam	Pleiku/Saigon
233*	7/22/70	Greece	Greece/Egypt
234*	7/25/70	Mexico	Mexico/Cuba
235	7/28/70	Argentina	Argentina/Cuba
236*	8/2/70	USA	USA/Cuba PAA
237	8/3/70	USA	West Germany/Hungary
238	8/7/70	Poland	Poland/West Germany
239*	8/8/70	Czechoslovakia	Czechoslovakia/Austria
240*	8/19/70	USA	USA/Cuba Trans Carib
241	8/19/70	Japan	Japan/possible suicide
242*	8/19/70	Poland	Poland/Denmark
243*	8/20/70	USA	USA/Cuba Delta
244*	8/24/70	USA	USA/Cuba TWA
245	8/26/70	Poland	Poland/Austria
246*	8/31/70	Algeria	Algeria/Yugoslavia
247*	9/6/70	USA	Germany/Jordan TWA
248*	9/6/70	Switzerland	Switzerland/Jordan Swissair
249*	9/6/70	USA	Netherlands/Egypt PAA
250	9/6/70	Israel	Netherlands/Jordan El Al
251*	9/9/70	U.K.	Bahrain/Jordan BOAC
252*	9/14/70	Rumania	Rumania/West Germany
253	9/15/70	USA	USA/North Korea TWA
254	9/16/70	Egypt	Egypt/Unknown
255*	9/19/70	Thailand	Thailand/North Vietnam
256*	9/19/70	USA	USA/Cuba Allegheny
257	9/27/70	U.K.	USA/Israel BOAC
258*	10/10/70	Iran	Iran/Iraq
259*	10/15/70	USSR	USSR/Turkey
260*	10/21/70	Costa Rica	Costa Rica/hostages held for lease of Costa Rican guerrillas
261*	10/27/70	USSR	USSR/Turkey
262*	10/30/70	USA	USA/Cuba National
263*	11/1/70	USA	USA/Cuba United
264*	11/9/70	Iran	Iran/Iraq
265	11/9/70	USSR	USSR/Sweden
266*	11/10/70	Saudi Arabia	Jordan/Iraq
267*	11/13/70	USA	USA/Cuba
268	12/21/70	USA	USA/Unknown

ttempt No.	*Date*	*Country Owning Aircraft*	*Departure/Arrival*
269*	1/3/71	USA	USA/Cuba Eastern
270	1/10/71	USA	USA/Unknown TWA
271*	1/22/71	Ethiopia	Ethiopia/Libya
272*	1/22/71	USA	USA/Cuba Northwest
273	1/23/71	South Korea	South Korea/Unknown
274	1/26/71	Dominican Republic	Dominican Republic/Cuba
275*	1/30/71	India	India/Pakistan
276*	2/4/71	USA	USA/Cuba Delta
277*	2/25/71	USA	USA/Canada Western
278	3/8/71	USA	USA/Canada National
279*	3/30/71	Philippines	Philippines/Chinese Peoples' Republic
280	3/31/71	USA	USA/Cuba Delta
281*	3/31/71	USA	USA/Cuba Eastern
282*	4/5/71	USA	USA/Cuba
283	4/13/71	Canada	Canada/Canada
284	5/13/71	Japan	Japan/North Korea
285	5/17/71	Sweden	Sweden/Unknown SAS
286	5/25/71	USA	USA/USA Air West
287*	5/27/71	Rumania	Rumania/Austria
288	5/28/71	USA	USA/Nassau Eastern
289*	5/29/71	USA	USA/Cuba PAA
290	6/4/71	USA	USA/Israel United
291	6/10/71	Philippines	Philippines/Unknown
292*	6/10/71	Unknown	Congo/Congo
293	6/11/71	USA	USA/North Vietnam TWA
294	6/18/71	USA	USA/Cuba Piedmont
295	6/29/71	Finland	Finland/Cuba
296	7/2/71	USA	USA/Algeria Braniff
297	7/11/71	Cuba	Cuba/Unknown
298	7/23/71	USA	USA/Italy TWA
299*	7/24/71	USA	USA/Cuba National
300	8/16/71	USA	USA/Unknown United
301	8/23/71	Egypt	Egypt/Israel
302	9/4/71	USA	USA/Cuba Eastern
303*	9/8/71	Jordan	Jordan/Libya
304	9/16/71	Jordan	Jordan/Unknown

Attempt No.	*Date*	*Country Owning Aircraft*	*Departure/Arrival*
305	9/24/71	USA	USA/Unknown American
306	10/4/71	Jordan	Jordan/Unknown
307	10/4/71	USA	USA/Bahamas
308*	10/9/71	USA	USA/Cuba
309*	10/10/71	Venezuela	Venezuela/Cuba
310	10/18/71	USA	USA/Cuba Wein Consolidated
311*	10/20/71	Ecuador	Ecuador/Cuba
312*	10/25/71	USA	USA/Cuba American
313	10/26/71	Greece	Greece/Italy
314*	11/3/71	Bolivia	Bolivia/Peru (theft versus hijacking)
315	11/12/71	Canada	Canada/Ireland
316	11/18/71	Trinidad	Trinidad/Canada
317*	11/24/71	USA	USA/USA NW
318*	11/27/71	USA	USA/Cuba TWA
319	12/4/71	France	France/E. Pakistan
320	12/13/71	Nicaragua	Nicaragua/Cuba
321	12/16/71	Bolivia	Bolivia/Bolivia
322	12/24/71	USA	USA/USA NW
323	12/26/71	USA	Canada/Cuba
324	12/26/71	USA	USA/USA AA
325*	1/7/72	USA	USA/Cuba (Africa?) PAS
326	1/12/72	USA	USA/S. America BR
327	1/20/72	USA	USA/(parachuted out of plane)
328	1/26/72	USA	USA/killed by FBI in Poughkeepsie, N.Y.
329*	1/27/72	USA	USA/Cuba
330	1/29/72	USA	USA/wounded and apprehended by FBI at JFK
331	2/18/72	Jordan	Egypt/Jordan
332*	2/21/72	Germany	India/Yemen
333*	3/7/72	USA	USA/Cuba
334	3/7/72	USA	USA/Sweden
335*	3/11/72	Italy	Italy/Germany
336*	3/19/72	USA	USA/Cuba
337*	3/21/72	Jamaica	Jamaica/Cuba
338	4/5/72	Indonesia	Indonesia/Extortion Attempt

Appendix IV Action Taken on Aviation Safety Treaties by Member Nations of the International Civil Aviation Organization *

Country	Sign Tokyo	Rat. Tokyo	Sign Hague	Rat. Hague	Sign Montreal	Rat. Montreal
Afghanistan						
Algeria						
Argentina	X	X	X		X	
Australia	X	X	X			
Austria			X			
Barbados	X		X		X	
Belgium	X	X	X		X	
Bolivia						
Brazil	X	X	X		X	
Bulgaria			X	X	X	
Burma						
Burundi	X	X	X			
Byelorussian Soviet Socialist Rep.			X		X	
Cameroon						
Canada	X	X	X		X	
Central African Republic						
Ceylon						
Chad	X	X			X	
Chile			X			
China, Republic of	X	X	X		X	
Columbia	X		X			
Congo, People's Republic of	X				X	
Costa Rica			X	X	X	
Cuba						
Cyprus						
Czechoslovakia			X		X	
Dahomey			X			
Denmark	X	X	X			
Dominican Republic	X	X	X			
Ecudaor	X	X	X	X		
El Salvador			X			
Ethiopia			X		X	
Federal Republic of Germany	X	X	X		X	
Finland	X	X	X			
France	X	X	X			
Gabon	X	X	X	X		

* ICAO is a specialized agency of the U.N.

Country	Sign Tokyo	Rat. Tokyo	Sign Hague	Rat. Hague	Sign Montreal	Rat. Montreal
Ghana			X			
Greece	X	X	X			
Guatemala	X	X	X			
Guinea			X			
Guyana						
Haiti						
Honduras						
Hungarian People's Republic	X	X	X	X	X	
Iceland	X	X				
India			X			
Indonesia	X		X			
Iran			X			
Iraq			X			
Ireland	X					
Israel	X	X	X	X	X	
Italy	X	X	X		X	
Ivory Coast	X	X				
Jamaica			X		X	
Japan	X	X	X	X		
Jordan			X			
Kenya	X	X				
Khmer Republic			X			
Kuwait			X			
Laos			X			
Lebanon						
Liberia	X					
Libyan Arab Republic						
*Liechtenstein	X	X				
Luxembourg			X			
Madagascar	X		X			
Malawi						
Malaysia			X			
Maldives						
Mali						
Malta						
Mauritania						
Mauritius						
Mexico	X	X	X			
Monaco						
USSR–Mongolia			X			
Morocco						
Nauru						
Nepal						
Netherlands	X	X	X		X	
New Zealand						
Nicaragua						
Niger	X	X	X			
Nigeria	X	X				
Norway	X	X	X	X		
Pakistan	X		X			

*Not ICAO member

Country	Sign Tokyo	Rat. Tokyo	Sign Hague	Rat. Hague	Sign Montreal	Rat. Montreal
Panama	X	X	X			
Paraguay	X	X	X			
People's Democratic Republic of Yemen						
People's Republic of the Congo						
Peru						
Philippines	X	X	X		X	
Poland	X	X	X		X	
Portugal	X	X	X		X	
Republic of Korea	X					
Republic of Viet-Nam						
Romania						
Rwanda	X	X	X			
San Marino						
Saudi Arabia	X	X				
Senegal	X		X		X	
Sierra Leone	X	X	X			
Singapore	X	X				
Somalia						
South Africa			X		X	
Spain	X	X	X			
Sudan						
Swaziland						
Sweden	X	X	X	X		
Switzerland	X	X	X	X	X	
Syria						
Thailand			X			
Togo	X	X				
Trinidad and Tobago			X			
Tunisia						
Turkey			X			
Uganda						
USSR–Ukraine					X	
Union of Soviet Socialist Republics			X		X	
United Arab Republic						
United Kingdom	X	X	X		X	
United Republic of Tanzania						
United States	X	X	X	X	X	
Upper Volta	X	X				
Uruguay						
Venezuela	X		X		X	
Yemen						
Yugoslavia	X	X	X		X	
Zambia						
TOTALS	**58**	**47**	**71**	**11**	**31**	**0**

Appendix V ICAO Treaties Concerning Skyjacking and Sabotage

TOKYO CONVENTION (1963) *Punishment of Offenses Committed on Board Aircraft*

The Tokyo Convention provides that the State of registration of the aircraft is competent to exercise jurisdiction of offenses committed on board. It empowers the aircraft commander to prevent the commission of such acts and disembark the person committing them. In event of unlawful and forcible seizure of an aircraft by a person on board, it obliges the States that are parties to it to release the passengers, crew, and aircraft immediately.

Although 26 nations signed the Convention on Sept. 14, 1963—thus signifying intent to ratify—only 13 signatories have filed ratification papers. Twelve ratifications were required to bring this treaty into force. It became effective Dec. 4, 1969. The U.S. did not ratify the treaty until 1969.

THE HAGUE CONVENTION (1970) *Suppression of Unlawful Seizure of Aircraft*

The Hague Convention calls for the return of the aircraft to control of its commander, assistance to passengers and crew for continuation of their journey, and apprehension and prosecution or extradition of the hijacker. Each contracting State agrees to make the offense punishable by severe penalties.

The Hague Convention was adopted 74 to 0 with two abstentions, and was signed by 50 of the 77 States attending the diplomatic conference. Finland signed after the treaty was opened for additional signatures on Jan. 1, 1971. The treaty became effective in October, 1971, with ratification by the required minimum of 10 States. Eleven nations had ratified as of November 1, 1971.

MONTREAL CONVENTION (1971) *For Suppression of Unlawful Acts of Interference Against Civil Aviation (other than hijacking)*

The Montreal Convention prescribes severe punishment for attacks against the lives of persons on board aircraft in flight, and for intentional acts, such as sabotage and bombings, that seriously damage aircraft or endanger safety of flight.

The Convention was signed in Montreal, Sept. 23, 1971, by 31 States. None had ratified as of November 1, 1971.

NOTE—Copies of the three documents above are available from the Secretary General of the International Civil Aviation Organization (ICAO), International Aviation Building, 1080 University Street, Montreal 101, Quebec, Canada.

Notes

Chapter One

1. The word "skyjacking" bothers the semantic purist because it is recently contrived and is considered journalese. But since hijacking a plane is a very different thing from hijacking a truck or a boat, "skyjack" seems a much more accurate word which immediately identifies the vehicle commandeered. Dr. David Hubbard in his book *The Skyjacker* suggests a different distinction between "hijacker" and "skyjacker." He defines a *hijacker* as a qualified pilot who flies or at least is competent to take over the controls of a stolen plane to cross a closed border; while the *skyjacker* is defined as a passive rider dependent on the skills of the flight crew he is forcing to take him to his destination.

2. During a psychiatric examination after being apprehended, the skyjacker explained his perplexing behavior—which *he* felt was quite rational. As a used car salesman (with what has to be an unprecedented feeling of responsibility to his customers) he returned from Mexico to wind up a number of unfinished deals. He was also concerned about his wife's sudden refusal to pack up the family and emigrate to Cuba. While back in the U.S. to clear up these problems, the FBI started making inquiries about parole violations (he had recently been released from prison; wrongly convicted, he claimed, for a crime engineered by his cousin). It was bitterness over this injustice that had prompted him to request Cuban citizenship. Realizing that

it was just a matter of hours before he would be apprehended by the authorities—compounding what he considered the initial injustice—he precipitously decided to skyjack, accompanied by his sixteen-year-old son.

3. While a significant number of skyjackings to Cuba have been accomplished by homesick Cubans who couldn't adjust to life in the United States, it is impossible to give an accurate count because identification and nationality of many of the Spanish-speaking skyjackers is still unknown. One thing that makes me question their mental balance is their penchant for illegal transportation across closed borders, since they risked their lives escaping from Cuba and repeated the risk on the return journey knowing that they would receive a chilly welcome and prison terms upon arrival back in Cuba. One Cuban refugee who defected to the United States was involuntarily returned to Havana by a skyjacker. George Prellezo was a captain with a Cuban airline when he hijacked his flight to Miami in 1960. He became a pilot with Southeast Airlines and was taking a flight out for a sick friend when his plane was skyjacked to Cuba in 1968. He was arrested when he arrived in Havana and Castro announced that Prellezo would be tried as a traitor facing the severest of penalties. The United States warned that he was now a U.S. citizen and demanded his release. Oddly enough, Castro had second thoughts about escalating the hostilities with the U.S. and allowed Prellezo to fly out of Cuba a free man—less than a month after his capture.

Chapter Two

1. Although the Palestinians are the most sensational of the political skyjackers, African, Latin American, and Japanese political dissidents have used skyjacking to embarrass their governments and publicize their causes.

2. The Popular Front for the Liberation of Palestine (PFLP) is an exile revolutionary organization based in Jordan with operations in all the Arab states where there are Palestinian refugee camps. Their prime commitment is to regain control of Palestine, using all the methods of guerrilla warfare. After the skyjackings in September of 1970, one high U.S. official in the State Department was reported to have said, "This proves that there can be no settlement of the Middle East problem without

the inclusion of the Palestinians in the negotiations." While this sounds like a sensible suggestion, so far no move has been made to bring the Palestinians to the conference table.

3. The International Federation of Air Line Pilots Association, angered at the refusal of the Algerians to release the flight crew, formally asked for a boycott of the Algerian airports on August 13, 1968. This threat prompted some speeding up of the negotiations, since Algeria was apparently not prepared to suffer such economic reprisals despite her commitment to the Palestinian cause. This was the second time IFALPA had used the threat of boycott on Algeria. On July 21, 1967, Moise Tshombe, former premier of the Congo, was flying in his British registered private plan to Majorca when one of his bodyguards forced the plane to Algeria where Tshombe was arrested and interned. The two British pilots, the passengers, and the plane were not released until September 22, 1967, after the Algerians had suddenly been persuaded to be more cooperative by IFALPA's threatened stoppage of all commercial flights in and out of Algeria.

4. One news item I came across in the International *Herald Tribune* the day after the skyjackings made me suspect that the Palestinians had some unique problems of their own with the reality principle. "A Palestinian guerrilla spokesman protested yesterday against the presence of armed guards on Israel's El Al Airlines flight as 'a gross violation of international law . . . speaking over Damascus radio in Syria, [he] said the failure of the guerrilla attempt to hijack an El Al Airliner near London Sunday was a result of the 'outrageous Israeli violation.'"

Chapter Three

1. *Reader's Digest* printed a featured condensation titled "This Is a Hijacking," by Jorg Andrees Elten, not long after the Palestinian exploits. It is a detailed, blow-by-blow description of the PFLP skyjackings which for sheer information about how to benefit from the mistakes of others is a major contribution to the revolutionary handbook. Politics makes strange bedfellows.

2. El Al regulations are that the two security guards are to be at their posts in the passenger compartment at all times. However, on this flight, one guard went into the cockpit for

take-off. The security guard and the pilot who allowed him in the cockpit were severely penalized by the airline when they returned to Israel.

3. One sky marshal who described his glamorous job with a rock record company apparently unduly impressed a passenger with his cover story. When asked what line of work *he* was in, the passenger leaned over and whispered, "You've heard of sky marshals?" The sky marshal nodded cautiously. "That's me," said the passenger.

4. The Customs Bureau released a bulletin on January 17, 1972, claiming that sky and ground marshals had seized 36,459 potentially lethal weapons during their first year of operation. I can't help feeling that this is an impressive but somewhat inflated statistic. I remember the cap gun taken from its ten-year-old owner, and the hundreds of pen knives and scissors I have been made the guardian of during my flights. One passenger laughingly noted that we had taken his old and blunt jacknife and then presented him with a metal knife twice as long and twice as sharp on his meal tray. Still, I suppose I would rather have overzealous searches than none at all.

The same report claimed that sky marshals had made twenty arrests on board the aircraft including seven in response to skyjacking threats. Knowing the idiotic jokes some passengers can make about skyjacking on flights, especially if they have had a little too much to drink, I wonder at the seriousness of the threats made by those seven passengers arrested in flight by the sky marshals. There is no detailed information available, but since the sky marshal program is fighting proposed budget cuts and desperately trying to justify its existence, any unfortunate drunk's mumbled joke will qualify him as a skyjacker. Potential jokesters should take this information to heart if they don't want to leave the plane in handcuffs.

5. Skyjackers are resorting to devilishly clever disguises for their weapons. A couple recently hid a gun in their baby's stroller. Another concealed his gun in a cast on his arm. On the other hand, I know of a perfectly innocent passenger with a metal plate in his head from a World War II injury who sets off the magnetometer—provoking a search—every time he flies.

Flying Scared

Chapter Eight

1. A telegram sent to Prime Minister Golda Meir by three U.S. crew members and twenty-six American passengers released by the PFLP after almost a month as hostages in Jordan reads:

> We condemn hijacking which imperils innocent citizens of all nations, but we understand that this was the PFLP's urgent attempt to bring their grievances before the world for a just review and a fair solution. We wish to affirm that our guards treated us humanely and always did their utmost to protect us against harm and to meet our basic needs.
>
> As free men and women, and in acknowledgment of our release, we urge you to make a reciprocal act signifying good will and offering new encouragement to Palestinian Arabs in the prospect of productive peace negotiations.

Half of the passengers who signed the telegram were American Jews.